China: The Reluctant Exodus

China: The Reluctant Exodus

by

Phyllis Thompson

HODDER AND STOUGHTON

and

THE OVERSEAS MISSIONARY FELLOWSHIP

British Library Cataloguing in Publication Data

Thompson, Phyllis
   China: The Reluctant Exodus. – (Hodder
Christian paperbacks).
   1. China Inland Mission – History
   1. Title
   266'.023'0951   BV3410

ISBN 0 340 24183 7

First published 1979

Copyright © 1979 by Phyllis Thompson

*Printed in Great Britain for
Hodder and Stoughton Ltd.,
Mill Road, Dunton Green, Sevenoaks, Kent
by C. Nicholls & Company Ltd.,
The Philips Park Press, Manchester*

Acknowledgements

I acknowledge with gratitude the help I have received from scores of former fellow-missionaries in China, who generously shared their experiences in response to my questions. They are too many to enumerate, but Dr. Rupert Clarke, Miss Lilian Fletcher, the late Mr. Arthur Mathews and Mr. Clarence Preedy come in for special mention. Miss May Price provided a fund of invaluable material in the form of letters written from C.I.M. headquarters during the critical years of 1950–52, and the Overseas Missionary Fellowship willingly gave permission to quote from their publications, as well as giving me access to their files. On the practical side I am deeply indebted to Miss Ruth Dix for providing me with a quiet place in which to write, in the sanctuary of her home, and Miss Mollie Robertson for so efficiently typing the MS.

In particular I am grateful to Mr. Arnold Lea, not only for the personal records he made available, but even more for the unfailing encouragement and wise suggestions with which he followed the progress of the MS.

PHYLLIS THOMPSON
LONDON
November 1978

Contents

Prologue

THE CONVOY WITH its two heavily-loaded lorries, two jeeps with trailers and a saloon car, was ready to depart. The headlights only served to accentuate the grey, early-morning mist that was turning into a thin drizzle of rain, but nothing could dim our enthusiasm. From my seat beside the driver in the second lorry I looked down on the crowd of well-wishers, Chinese and westerners, who were there to see us off, and waved an excited goodbye. We were all eager to get away now, to leave the ordered security of the large Mission compound in Sinza Road, and strike the trail for Chungking and the west. The engines purred as one by one the vehicles moved slowly out through the great gates and turned into the cosmopolitan streets of Shanghai.

It was an exhilarating moment, for the vehicles in which we travelled contained three and a half tons of Bibles, one of the largest consignments to go into China since the end of World War Two. The warning we had received that there were possible dangers on the road because of sporadic fighting between Chinese Nationalists and Communist guerillas only added zest to the adventure. When had there not been dangers in travel, anyway? Onward Christian soldiers! This was the golden Gospel age of China, the halcyon period of open doors and open hearts. Students in universities were forming Christian fellowships, the Pocket Testament League was distributing hundreds of thousands of Gospels to the armed forces, ardent young evangelists were holding meetings in prisons, and reports from all quarters told of an unusual responsiveness to the good news of the Kingdom of God. Pioneer work was forging ahead, too. On the mountainous western borders

workers who had been held back during the long years of
the war were pressing forward at last, with Dr. Jim Broomhall leading his team into the perilous territory of Independent Nosu-land, Dr. Rupert Clarke opening a medical
clinic among Tibetans, and surveys under way in the
south-west in search of the tribes that were still without a
witness to Christ.

True, ominous clouds were gathering over the northern
horizon, and already some Mission centres were being
evacuated as steely, well-disciplined Communist regiments
pitted themselves against the Nationalist army. But the
two mighty rivers that flowed from west to east right across
China had to be crossed and held before the Communists
could gain control of the whole land. 'It'll take them ten
years, if they can do it at all,' asserted the optimists, 'and
even then they've got the Chinese temperament to contend
with!' The Chinese with their deep-seated family loyalty,
ingrained through several millenia, how could the State expect to take control of their minds in a mere decade?
'Communism can never conquer the Chinese.'

So we tried to believe as the Bible convoy threaded its
way through the thickly-populated provinces south of the
Yangtze, crossing rivers on ferry-boats, chugging along the
pot-holed roads in the agricultural plains, grinding up
snake-like roads that wound over mountains. However
dark might be the picture in the northern provinces where
the Communists had entrenched themselves, the picture
elsewhere was bright indeed. There was no opposition to
the open air meetings we held along the way, nor restrictions to impede us. Outstretched hands eagerly grasped
the tracts we held out in the vociferous markets. 'Wonderful openings!' we said to each other. 'They're so ready to
listen. This is the day of opportunity, if ever there was
one!'

It was not only that the doors stood wide open for the
western missionary in areas that were freed again after the
Japanese invasion. There was something deeper than that.

An inward glow was animating the Church in China. The Little Flock and the Jesus Family were no products of western Christianity imported by missionaries. They were indigenous, and the vitalising if disturbing influences of their example and teaching was being felt far and wide. Men like Watchman Nee in Shanghai and Wang Ming Tao in Peking were not only preaching with power, but writing with power, too. Chinese Christian writers for Chinese readers at last! And the spirit of evangelism was abroad in an unprecedented way, urging young people to set off for faraway regions, right to the very limits of their own land, venturing out in response to an unquenchable conviction that God was sending them to take the news about His Son to those whose right it was to hear. 'It is our inheritance, and we must claim it!' was the challenge, and they were rising to it. In every place I went to I met them – a nurse from Tientsin and a young business man from Shanghai in a town on the Tibetan border, an ardent young student from a Pentecostal Bible School whose Hallelujahs shattered the early morning silence in a city in the far west, four charming but self-possessed young women evangelists from Manchuria who arrived unheralded in a city near Inner Mongolia. Several members of a little Chinese missionary society in Lanchow, the gateway to Central Asia, were scattering north and west. 'The Back to Jerusalem Band' we called them, for their hope was to carry the Gospel right across central Asia, back to Jerusalem from where it was first sounded forth.

It was fresh and it was inspiring. There was something apostolic about it, this spontaneous upsurge of ardour and dedication that owed nothing to man-planned organisations, revealing itself simultaneously in Christian groups quite unrelated to each other. Surely it all augured an era in which the Word of God would be sounded clear and loud throughout the land?

Yet less than three years later I was on my way back to Shanghai with a one-way travel permit knowing I was leaving never to return. Down through a strangely silent China I journeyed, in which unsmiling officials scrutinised my papers suspiciously, so that it was with considerable surprise I learned that my request to stop off in the city of Kaifeng for thirty-six hours was granted. In that brief time I hoped to meet once more some of those who had been fellow-workers in the Gospel during the war.

One had been an evangelist, well-known and loved in the churches on the plain. Now he was working in the hospital, employed like everyone else by the State. Calm-eyed and smiling he came forward to greet me, tall and upright as ever, unchanged but for one thing. The hair that had been jet black had turned to grey.

'What is it like for you, working under the Communists?' I asked in a low voice. Somehow one spoke softly, even though no potential informer was near.

For answer he held his hands apart, fingers outspread, as though gripping an invisible object. Then slowly, inexorably, he brought his hands together, and as I looked, I understood. Whatever was held between those hands was being crushed.

'It's like that,' he said quietly. Then he added, 'But the Lord is with us.' And I knew that something indestructible was there.

Phyllis Thompson

CHAPTER ONE

Shanghai: 1948

THE CLICKING SOUND of typewriters along the office corridor rose and fell spasmodically, sometimes rising to a crescendo of feverish haste, sometimes fading altogether as doors opened and anxious faces peered out, looking questioningly towards the China Director's office. Any important news would be duly pinned up on the notice board for all to see, but one might get it a little earlier if one happened to be around at the right moment. The Secretary, the Treasurer, the Regional Directors were in and out of the room all the time, emerging unsmiling to dictate urgent letters or hurry off on some official business. Things weren't going well, that was obvious, and everyone was affected. The tension of suspense communicated itself to all.

J.R.S.* himself sat at his desk, trim and unflappable as ever, only the rather grim set of his lips and the furrows on his forehead betraying his disquiet. Not that he ever tried to disguise it, or put on a show of confidence he did not feel. 'You know where you are with J.R.S.' If he was worried about anything he said so, and he was worried now.

A shock of horror had run through the whole missionary body in China when the news leaked through that Miss Lenell of the Swedish Mission, who had been living in a region under Communist domination for some time, had been suddenly arrested, tried by a People's Tribunal, and executed. Such a thing had never happened before. Missionaries had been killed in riots, murdered by bandits,

* J.R.S. John Robertson Sinton, China Director of C.I.M.

died as prisoners of war, but this show of justice resulting in execution 'by the will of the people' was new—and ominous. When J.R.S. heard of it he caught his breath ejaculating, 'Poor woman!' Then his mind flew to the members of C.I.M. who were up north, near that troubled territory, who would stay there until he told them to move out. That was always the general directive. One didn't cut and run any time things looked dangerous. One waited for instructions to do so, and they came from the Superintendent of one's district, or the Director of one's region, and the final responsibility rested with the General Director. If the General Director was out of the country and emergencies arose demanding prompt action, the China Director, his deputy, had to take control. That was the position J.R.S. found himself in now, and he didn't like it.

The execution of Miss Lenell was followed by further alarms, as in rapid succession word was received of the death by violence of four members of other missions in various parts of the country. That those in the China Inland Mission, largest and most widely spread of all the Protestant missions in China, had so far escaped was a matter for thankfulness, but nothing could be taken for granted. The C.I.M. was as vulnerable as any other, and none of its members must be left in territory that was clearly under Communist control. The problem that faced the men on Headquarters Staff in Shanghai each time a letter or a telegram, a phone call or a radio broadcast gave news of a further Communist advance was to assess whether it would be temporary or permanent.

'Communists occupied part of Shensi, then retreated again.'

'Nationalists holding Anking, but communication difficult.'

'No news from the Andersons in Shekichen for weeks. Nothing getting through.'

'Communists over the Yellow River!'

Refugees were pouring south now, towns on the railroad were alive with them. The Communists advanced again in Shensi, hundreds were flooding out of Sian the capital, panic-stricken.

Alarm followed alarm.

'Communists beginning to concentrate on Kaifeng .. The railway between Hsuchow and Kaifeng has been cut!'

Kaifeng! The capital of Honan, it was without natural defences once the Yellow River was crossed. If Kaifeng were threatened the whole province would be affected, for the vast agricultural plain would present few military problems. The uppermost thought in his mind now was the Mission hospital, where the work was flourishing under the leadership of Dr. Vaughan Rees*. Henry Guinness, whose father founded the hospital some fifty years ago, was sending enthusiastic reports of the warmth of spiritual fellowship among the staff, and of the unprecedented stream of conversions to Christ among the patients. Must all this be put in jeopardy now?

In sombre mood J.R.S. gathered his staff around him.

'We've got to come to a decision about the Kaifeng hospital,' he said. 'It's no good waiting until the Communists are attacking the city to decide whether we'll be able to keep the hospital open. You can't close a hospital overnight. The patients – the staff – the medicines – the equipment – the premises ... What's to be done?'

It was the gravest problem they'd had to deal with yet. A hospital provides a social service to the whole community, irrespective of creed or ideology, and this one, the oldest of the four C.I.M. hospitals in China was known and respected over a very wide area. Hospitals were needed whatever government was in power, and to close this one down would add greatly to the general distress and dismay. Yet what was the alternative? The UNRRA medical team that had helped in its rehabilitation after the Japanese were defeated had been withdrawn more than a year ago. The missionaries in charge must not remain in Communist

* Author of *The Jesus Family in Communist China*.

occupied territory, and there seemed little likelihood that the Nationalists could hold out much longer. That would leave a hospital complete with staff and equipment, but with no-one to run it, and the result could be chaotic. Better to close it down in an orderly way now than to leave it suddenly in a last minute rush.

Telegrams were sent to the missionaries in Kaifeng instructing them to terminate the hospital work. No more patients were to be admitted. Those already in the wards must be sent home, and the staff given notice. The hospital must be closed. There was no alternative.

At this point, however, another plan began to unfold, as the removal of scaffolding reveals a solid building. It became evident that, after all, there was an alternative. The Chinese leaders of the District Council of Churches, with its ramifications throughout the whole region, came forward with the suggestion that they should take over the hospital. They were prepared to take full responsibility. They could only do it in a modified way, but if the Mission were willing to hand it over, they were willing to accept it. Dr. Lin, known throughout the district for his Christian testimony as well as his medical skill, had received his own training in this hospital, and he loved it. He was willing to become its Superintendent.

This unexpected proposal transformed the situation. Instead of jettisoning the hospital it could be handed over to a responsible body of men who would do their best to ensure that its Christian standards were maintained. When and if the Communists took the city, it would be functioning normally, but as an institution belonging to the Chinese church, not to a western missionary society.

Basically the proposition was completely in line with the policy of the Mission, formulated twenty years before, that the churches should become

Self-governing

Self-supporting

Self-propagating

It had taken a political upheaval, when in 1927 a storm of anti-foreign feeling had driven hundreds of missionaries from their centres inland to the security of the Treaty Ports, to bring about a drastic evaluation of missionary methods. What will happen to our churches if we can't get back? had been the searching question many had asked then, and the honest answer had been that in most cases they would probably peter out. They were too dependent on the missionary for oversight, for support, and for inspiration, and were quite unprepared to shoulder responsibility and take the lead.

The outcome of all the discussions and heart-searching of those days had been a radical change of attitude towards the task of extending the Kingdom of God in China. When eventually things had quietened down again and missionaries were able to return inland, those in the C.I.M. had the difficult task of introducing and implementing the 'Three Self' policy on their own stations.

Self-governing meant the Chinese Christians learned to look to God direct, rather than to the missionary, for decisions in church matters.

Self-propagating meant they should initiate their own evangelistic efforts and Bible-teaching programmes. The missionary was there to co-operate and help, but no longer to lead.

Self-supporting meant that they should provide their own finance, not look to the Mission for the money to support pastors and Biblewomen, evangelists and teachers.

The process of weaning the churches from dependence on the Mission had been a long and painful one, but the end had been achieved. Pastors and church workers were supported by their own congregations, not from Mission funds. Bible Schools maintained by the Mission were giving place to those initiated and maintained by Chinese Christians, in which missionaries were merely members of the faculty. Things had been moving in the right direction, but for a District Council of Churches to come forward at such a time as this, and be prepared to shoulder the whole responsibility for running a hospital, was more than a step. It was a leap! Who but God could have foreseen, twenty years before, that it would be necessary, and who but He could have made it possible?

'We must hand over to them legally, and as soon as we can,' it was agreed. 'It will mean the hospital can be kept open and its Christian witness continued. They're good men. God bless them! They don't know what they're taking on, but He does, and He won't fail them.'

The transaction was completed, the missionaries were withdrawn, but the hospital remained open.

Meanwhile the civil war continued to ebb and flow – but it flowed more than it ebbed. Towns were attacked and occupied as the Communists advanced, then retreated, then advanced again and held their positions. Fighting in country areas increased as the Nationalist Government weakened, their pitiful, underpaid, conscripted soldiers no match for the disciplined, dedicated bands of Communists who, proclaiming themselves liberators, behaved towards the common people with restraint and even courtesy, paying good money for their food and actually returning things they borrowed. The common people knew little about politics or ideologies, but they knew when their grain was paid for and when it wasn't, who returned their spades after use and who went off with them. However cruelly the Communist-inspired bands of guerillas had behaved during the years of the war, they were being brought under firm control now. Secret sympathisers abounded, ready to welcome 'the liberators' as soon as they arrived.

Kaifeng was taken. The Communists retreated after a few days, and when Henry Guinness visited the city later he found the hospital functioning satisfactorily, though in a more limited way.

'The Lord has given us two things,' Dr. Lin told him, 'Unity of heart and unity of purpose. We want Christ to be glorified.' Whether under a Nationalist or a Communist government, that was their aim.

It was the last time he saw them. The Communist advanced again, and this time they did not retreat.

*   *   *

'Should we think about setting up a skeleton H.Q. in Chungking again?' J.R.S. asked himself as he watched the trend of events through those momentous days of 1948, conscious that the Nationalists were crumbling, that the country was being carved up. The possibility had to be faced that some areas might be cut off from Shanghai. There was something about the situation that was strangely reminiscent of the war years, when the setting up of a skeleton headquarters in Chungking, which sprang instantly into operation when Shanghai was immobilised after the Japanese attack on Pearl Harbour, had ensured that the Mission in Free China had continued working without a hitch. He'd been at the helm then, sifting and weighing the uncertain reports about Japanese advances to make sure that no-one else was caught unawares. But at least he had been in a China united against a common foe. Now it was in a state of civil war.

'A skeleton H.Q. in Chungking?' He talked about it and prayed about it with the men on H.Q. staff. God had undoubtedly directed that way during the War, when no-one else had forseen the dramatic turn of events. Was He indicating the same course of action again?

'Wouldn't it be a good idea also to have a financial centre ready right outside China?' someone suggested. 'Hongkong is on the doorstep, but as a British Crown Colony is outside the jurisdiction of any Chinese government, whether Nationalist or Communist. In an emergency, funds could be sent there from the homelands and drafted to any part of China – Shanghai or Chungking.'

They had no idea how vital was to be the decision that they made then. At the time it was merely a safeguard to

ensure that anyone in the Mission in China could draw
money, even if temporarily cut off from Headquarters.
And as it was much more economical to produce Chinese
Christian literature in Hongkong than in China, Mr. and
Mrs. Kenneth Price were appointed there for that work.

'But in the event of Shanghai being temporarily cut off
from any other part of the field, Mr. Price would make it
his business to supply the area with funds as long as the
emergency lasted.' The whole Mission was notified of this
move, though it was not implied that such an emergency
could be anything but temporary. The Communists were
proving an unexpectedly formidable force, advancing more
rapidly than anyone had anticipated, but their victories
were mainly in the remoter, under-developed regions.

The Nationalists might be harassed and communications
cut, but they could hold their own for a long time yet.

Then, at the end of October, the civil war in China
suddenly became headline news all round the world.

Mukden, an important junction on the Trans-Siber-
ian railway on the border of Manchuria, was occupied by
the Communists, and the Nationalists were in full retreat.
There was nothing now to stop the inflow of arms and aid
from the Soviet Union to support the Chinese Communists.

The effect of the advantage gained was shattering. Within a week the Nationalist Cabinet had resigned, Chinese
currency fell dramatically on the world money market, and
there was a panic-stricken rush of wealthy Chinese to get
out of China while the going was good.

At this point, to his great relief, J.R.S. received a cable
from the General Director offering to return to China immediately. He cabled back an immediate reply in the affir-
mative, for his earnest desire was to have his leader back at
the helm. By mid-December Bishop Houghton was back
in Shanghai, to hold one of the most momentous meetings
of Headquarters Staff the Mission had ever known. Those
present were never likely to forget it.

As always, it was opened with prayer. Then, in an expectant yet restrained silence, they listened as the tall, slim, sensitive man who must take the final responsibility for decisions made, outlined the situation as he saw it.

There was the probability now that a Communist Government would be set up in those parts of China where they had gained control. Heads bowed imperceptibly, but in agreement.

A Government would wish to maintain international contacts, he continued, and for that reason would have some respect for foreign opinions. It would not now be likely to act with the irresponsibility of an invading army towards foreigners holding bona fide passports issued by their governments.

J.R.S. sat immovable. A case was being built up – where would it lead?

There were evidences that the Communist leaders' policy towards missionaries had changed ...

Dubious murmurs from his listeners evoked the quick explanation that though their fundamental attitudes towards the Gospel remained the same, expediency in the present circumstances was affecting their actions.

'We have yet to prove that Christian witness will be impossible under a Communist Government in China ...

'The Gospel is intended for the whole world, including those who have come under the sway of Communism ...

'God called us to serve Him in China – has He withdrawn that call?'

It was evident now what it was all leading up to. What the General Director was proposing was that the Mission should be prepared to remain on in China, even under a Communist Government.

Tongues were loosened then. Arguments for and against the proposal were freely expressed, but the over-riding argument was the call of God, re-affirmed through the man they all acknowledged as their leader. The outcome of the meeting was the unanimous decision to withdraw no

more workers from areas in danger of Communist invasion
and occupation. Those in the provinces next in line of
attack would be advised to remain at their posts. If they
wished to withdraw they could do so, but it would mean
resigning from the Mission.

All members were informed of the new policy, and as
they read on they came to the words:

'If the conditions made it impossible to do effective
work, or if the degree of risk to life was high (it is not our
business carelessly to throw our lives away) we should
think differently.' Then came the challenging reminder,
'While we do not court danger, we are committed to a life
which may involve it.'

No-one could foresee what strain and suffering would
result from that momentous decision to withdraw no
more from living under a Communist regime in China.
Even had they known, however, there were very few who
would have reacted in any other way than to follow instructions and 'stay put'. Their Master had never
promised them the way would be easy.

CHAPTER TWO

South Wind Blows Softly

ARNOLD LEA paused at a bend in the age-old path with its worn, shallow steps to wipe his face with the towel around his neck, and look back at the city of Chungking, built on the steeply rising hill opposite the one he was climbing, and down on the full, surging water of the Yangtze that lay between. He'd be over the ridge in a few minutes now, among the trees and the flat-roofed houses scattered along the hillside, back in the old familiar courtyard with its view over the vast plain that he knew so well. Strange, the way history was repeating itself. Less than ten years ago the Mission's emergency headquarters had been established up here, and many was the time he had crossed the river and walked, perspiring, over the ridge to talk his problems over with J.R.S.

The big difference between then and now, he said to himself with a wry grin, was that J.R.S. was out of reach in Shanghai and he, Arnold Lea, was the one to whom people were coming with their problems. He didn't feel he had all the answers, not by a long way!

He had been sent to Chungking to set up an emergency H.Q. only a few days before Shanghai was taken by the Communists. Even as he and Jeannie had been boarding the Lutheran Mission's plane, the St. Paul, they had heard the sound of guns thundering in the distance. Within a week Shanghai had fallen and he'd found himself the focal point of the widely distributed members of the Mission in those parts of China still in the hands of the Nationalists. It had not been long before he'd asked Rowland Butler to come

and join him and share the burden of this unexpected responsibility. Rowland's faith was linked to a very good
head for business, and Arnold felt the need of someone like
that alongside. Actually, things had gone more smoothly
than might have been expected, largely due to the fore-
sight in setting up that little centre in Hongkong, from
which funds could be sent equally easily into Nationalist or Communist territory.

Arnold's concern just now was to rent enough bungalows to house the new missionaries due to arrive in the
autumn. Forty-nine of them were expected, from the
U.S.A. and Canada, Britain and South Africa, Australia
and New Zealand. Arriving in 1949, they were inevitably
called 'the 49ers'. Fine young people, to judge by the
reports sent from the home countries, eager to come in
spite of the fact that not a few other Missions were pulling
out of China, and that Americans were being urged by their
Consulate to leave the country. The new policy of C.I.M.
to remain on in China, even if it meant doing so under a
Communist Government, had come in for some criticism
in various circles, and that was not surprising. The strong
inward conviction of the C.I.M. leaders that it was in
God's plan for them to do so, however, left them with no
alternative. It was a case of 'business as usual', and that
included making the usual arrangements for an annual
language school for new workers. The last group of new
workers were still cooped up in Shanghai, waiting to get
out to the provinces, so it had been decided that this year's
contingent should come to the west, where travelling was
unrestricted.

The Mission's holiday bungalows up in these hills were
to become the new language school – and very nice too,
thought Arnold, away from the heavy humid heat that enveloped him in the city. It was an ideal place for young
people to get acclimatised while they applied their minds
to language study and with Marvin and Miriam Dunn in
charge he knew they'd get a good introduction to life as

missionaries in China. Marvin Dunn's career had been faced with the challenge of danger and sacrifice very early, for John Stam, with whom he had travelled out to China, had been publicly executed, two years later, by the then outlawed Communists, along with his wife Betty. Their martyrdom had made world missionary news.* Later Marvin had gone to work in the very town where his friends had laid down their lives. It was from there he set out on a journey that involved escorting a young missionary nurse through mountains where bandits lurked, and one night their inn was broken into, and having been stripped of all their valuables, including the nurse's medical equipment, they were left roped together with little left but the clothes they were wearing.

That incident had a happy ending, for the knot with which they were tied together proved to be prophetic, and they were married a year later. Their fruitful work in Anhwei province had been cut short by the Japanese invasion, but before returning home on furlough they had seen the end of the war, and taken charge of the first group of new workers to arrive in China from Britain. A first-rate couple to head up the language school in these hazardous days! Arnold had no misgivings about them, and it was a relief to know they would soon be arriving to take charge of the necessary arrangements.

Meanwhile, other matters were pressing on his mind. The mountainous areas of the south-west were in a turmoil. Brigandage was rife. Whether the brigands were Communists as they claimed, or whether they were just taking advantage of the general unrest mattered little. 'The Reds' were a law to themselves, and a danger to anyone who crossed their path. Sometimes weeks passed without any communication being received from missionaries living in those regions – Allan and Evelyn Crane, for instance, living among the Lisu and Lahu tribal Christians in that remote autonomous Shan state near the Burma border.

*The Triumph of John and Betty Stam by Mrs. Howard Taylor.

Nothing had been heard of them for months, and there was no way of knowing whether the letters sent to them ever got through.

As it happened, the Cranes' only contact with the outside world was what they heard over their radio, and it brought them small comfort, since the news was all of fierce and increasingly widespread fighting and they wondered what was happening to their two girls in the Mission's school for missionary children in the delightful hill resort of Kuling in Kiangsi. For months they had been without letters from anyone, for the Post Offce had ceased to function when the Chinese officials fled. Then the chief Shan prince had escaped into Burma, leaving the tribal villagers to protect themselves against 'the Reds' as best they could. After seven or eight weeks of sleeping in a shack in the jungle the Cranes decided they were too much of a burden on the Lisu Christians who were protecting them, and providing them with their food as well. They took the dangerous journey over the mountains, escorted by fifty tribesmen, narrowly escaping capture by the Shan soldiers and local 'Reds', and slipped over the border into Burma. Only then were they able to get in touch with Headquarters, and learn that their daughters were in excellent health and that the school in Kuling was continuing as usual.

By that time others in the tribal regions were being affected. 'The Reds' were rampaging unpredictably, and John Kuhn had to make a difficult decision as the time approached for the field conference of Yunnan workers to be held in Paoshan. Could he leave Isobel alone in the Lisu village that was six days' journey over the mountains to the nearest motor road while he went to attend the conference?

'You must go. You're the superintendent and you're needed there. The Lord will look after me. And we know we can trust the Lisu. You must go!' That was Isobel's attitude, and in the end he went.

While he was in Paoshan the Communists captured the city, and he was unable to leave.

* * *

Rowland Butler was in Chungking when he heard that Kweiyang in Kweichow was next in the line of Communist advance. That was his city, the centre from which he had travelled all over the province visiting the missionaries for whom he, as superintendent, was responsible.

'I must get back to them,' he told Arnold, who agreed. 'Can't leave them there with no-one to turn to in all the unknown crises that may develop under a new regime.' The return journey was going to be a bit difficult, for both his wife and two-year-old son had whooping cough, but they set out anyway, taking with them another missionary whose husband was in Kweiyang. It was five p.m. by the time they were ready to start, and a mist was already falling. But they were greatly encouraged by the reading in *Daily Light* for that day:

> '*He led them on safely . . .*'
> '*Behold, I send an Angel before thee, to keep thee in the way, and to bring thee into the place which I have prepared . . .*'

The long journey overland lay through bandit-infested mountains, and over broken bridges, all in thick fog. They rested for a couple of hours after midnight, then pressed on again, only stopping when somewhat bedraggled figures blocked their way, carrying rifles. They were not bandits, but retreating Nationalist soldiers, who cast covetous eyes at the 'carry-all' as they called the car. They wanted to requisition it, but whooping cough has a way of making its presence heard, and the soldiers reluctantly stood back. It would have been 'without human feeling' to deprive a woman and a child who were obviously suffering from it, of their means of getting home. The Butler party was allowed to go on, eventually reaching Kweiyang late in the evening. They entered a city that was ominously quiet. The Nationalists had departed, and the populace, behind closed doors, was apprehensively awaiting the arrival of the Communists.

The Butler's, a couple of days later, listening to Peking radio news as they sat peacefully eating their breakfast, were somewhat amused to hear that fierce fighting had been taking place in Kweiyang, culminating in a decisive victory for the People's Liberation Army, who were now entering the city to the welcoming cheers of the inhabitants.

*   *   *

The picture was very similar in many places, with the Nationalists retreating two or three days before the Communists arrived. Two young missionaries awoke from a good night's sleep to learn that 'the liberators' were at the gates. Within a short time some soldiers wearing the battle-green tunics of the P.L.A. were seen bearing aloft white flags of peace, and announcing that everything would continue just as before – including freedom of worship. In another place the first evidence most people had of their arrival was to see red flags being openly displayed over some of the houses. In yet another, the early morning light revealed P.L.A. sentries quietly patrolling the deserted streets.

For Alfred Bosshardt their arrival revived traumatic memories, for less than twenty years before they had arrived in very different circumstances, as the ruthless, bedraggled, indomitable Eighth Route Army, revolutionaries who were prepared to die for their cause, but never surrender. They had taken Alfred Bosshardt off as a hostage then, and for nearly two nightmarish years he had been forced to trail along with them over the mountains, sharing their hardships and enduring their brutalities. His faith in God had been tried in the crucible during those years, but deepened and encouraged too, as he had proved the power of God's hand to restrain, to provide, and to deliver. Emaciated, in rags, but smiling, he was eventually sent away to freedom riding on a donkey. He and his wife had returned to the home countries for a period of recuperation during which thousands of people had been moved by the relating of his story. Then they had calmly gone back to China, to the very province where he had experienced so much suffering.

But how would he react to the suggestion that he should again submit to Communist control? That was the question raised early in the solemn discussions in C.I.M. Headquarters in Shanghai when it was decided to remain on. 'What about Bosshardt?' He'd been through so much already! Was it right to ask him to face the uncertainties of a Communist regime when his memories of the past must be so harrowing? Bishop Houghton felt the responsibility keenly, and a special letter went to the Bosshardts explaining that theirs was realised to be an exceptional case, and if they wished to leave before the P.L.A. reached their city, it would be well understood. However, the Bosshardts prayed about it, and came to the conclusion that they should remain on.

'Eventually the K.M.T.* left our city and for three days we were without officials, waiting for the coming of the new government. A welcome was arranged for the newcomers and I found myself among the advance welcoming party! They did not arrive until after nightfall,' he wrote later, 'the change-over was so quiet and the soldiers so well-behaved they immediately made a good impression.' But he added, 'It was a weird feeling to be back again under Red Control.'

The whole country was coming under Communist domination far more quickly than most people had anticipated. With the north-east firmly in their control they had plunged south, occupying Nanking in April and Shanghai

* Kuo Min Tang. The Nationalist Army.

in May. Consolidating their positions in these areas they had advanced again, this time in the north-west. In August the strategically placed city of Lanchow fell to them, and the following month General Mao Tse Tung officially announced the establishment of the People's Republic of China with its capital in Peking. In October the fall of Canton to the P.L.A. meant that the south-east was virtually all under their control.

When the news came that Kweiyang had changed hands, Marvin and Miriam Dunn realised it was only a matter of time before Chungking would change hands, too. The murmur of distant gunfire had been heard even as the new missionaries from England were disembarking from the Lutheran plane, St. Paul, in which they had been flown from Hongkong. There had been no other way to come. Overland routes were closed to them.

Meanwhole the murmer of gunfire was changing to a more articulate mutter as the fighting drew nearer and nearer. Marvin awoke long before daylight on 29 November, and slipped immediately out of bed, dressed hurriedly, and went out. The quiet hillside was shrouded in a soft mist, and no-one was astir in the bungalows scattered among the trees. Some eighty people, missionaries, language teachers and servants were asleep in those bungalows, and he was responsible for providing money and provisions for them all.

One thought was uppermost in his mind as he set off briskly down the hill side to the ferry that would take him across the river to the city. Money! He *must* get hold of money, and it must be either gold bars or silver dollars. Paper money was practically worthless now. As in the days of the war, when inflation soared like an air-borne balloon, it was losing value from the moment you brought it out of the bank, great bundles of it, and put it in the rickshaw you had to hire to carry it home. Only precious metal had any lasting value. Gold bars, he thought, were out of the question now. Even silver dollars were almost unprocurable, but there must be some to be obtained, somewhere. With a prayer in his heart, and the astute Mr. Wang, a business man, by his side, he hurried towards Chungking. Maybe they'd find someone who would produce carefully hidden silver dollars in exchange for a cheque on a bank in Hongkong, where its value would be paid out in good foreign currency.

Had he foreseen what the day was to hold for those he left behind, he would almost certainly not have gone.

The day started in the usual way, and by nine a.m. the language students were divided into small groups with the Chinese teachers. Max and Joan Orr were at their desks. Before the first period was over, however, the familiar sound of gunfire started up, perceptibly nearer, sharp, strong, sustained. Apprehensive glances were exchanged, whispered consultations held, then Max said, 'I think we'd better give up the classes today.' He was apparently unruffled. He hailed from Belfast, and was not the excitable type. 'Go back to your own houses – and stay indoors!'

There was a quick gathering up of books, and the students and teachers disappeared, scuttling off along the mountain paths that led to their various bungalows. The compound was deserted now, and Faith Leeuwenburg, who did the catering, hurried along the verandah in the bungalow she shared with the Dunns, to find Miriam and the children. 'Let's play inside,' she said cheerfully, and they went into the dining room. The shooting continued, getting nearer all the time, then they heard the sound of running footsteps and some loud shouts of command. On the little knoll behind the kitchen a group of Nationalist soldiers were setting up a machine-gun!

Quickly the two women ran to close the wooden shutters at the window, then looked round for a safe place for the children. The lathe and plaster of their bungalow would be poor protection against flying bullets. 'Wouldn't you like to pretend you're hiding in a cave?' The children must not be frightened. 'That would make a good game. You three get under the table, and we'll cover it over, and you'll really be in a cave ...!' Cover the table with blankets, quick! That rug ... the quilt ...! 'Why, Auntie Faith, where are the children? I can't see them!' Her heart thudding, Miriam managed to keep her voice steady. 'Where can they be?'

The gunfire increased, menacingly, and the two women moved closer to each other. They tried to pray, but somehow words would not come.

Then another sound arrested them. It came from within the room itself, a muffled sound from under the table. A child's voice, singing.

> 'Jesus loves me, this I know
>   For the Bible tells me so,
> Little ones to Him belong
>   They are weak, but He is strong ...'

Miriam and Faith, their eyes suddenly wet, looked at each other and smiled.

'Jesus loves – *us*' murmured Miriam, a little choke in her voice. 'We are weak, but He is strong ... We don't need to be afraid!' The tension was broken, by a little child singing in the dark.

Then they realised that the machine-gun had ceased firing 'Listen!' whispered Faith. 'It's stopped – what's happened?' Peeping through the shutter slats they saw that the hillock was empty. The Nationalists had withdrawn, taking their gun with them. The sharp patter of bullets continued from down the valley, however, getting nearer. The Communists were mounting the hillside, and the path ran right past the house where the nine Chinese language teachers lived.

Suddenly silence fell. The gunfire had ceased. Looking out through the shutters the two women held their breath as they saw the Chinese teachers walking up the path, hands held over their heads, soldiers in battle-green uniforms with red stars blazing from their caps coming behind them, rifles at the ready . . .

*   *   *

For all in the Language School it was an unforgettable morning, as they lived through the experience of being right in the line of fire between two opposing military forces. The girls in one bungalow watched helplessly as a machine-gun was set up on their varandah, manned by a few Nationalist soldiers, who sent showers of bullets raining down the hillside. A macabre touch was added by the line of washing hanging up to dry, through which the bullets went whistling.

Max Orr, going to a window in his house, looked out into the eyes of a soldier with a red star in his green cap, who was startled as he at what he saw. The Communist had not been expecting to see the face of a white man. It took some time to convince him that no Nationalist soldiers were being sheltered inside.

One of the girl students, venturing out on the verandah nearly ran on to the fixed bayonet of a man in battle green, who was obviously as surprised as she was at the unexpected encounter. The same sort of thing occurred at other bungalows, but once a search had been made the Communist officers called their men off. 'You will be safe here,' they said reassuringly. 'We will not hurt you. We must go on and find the Nationalist men . . .'

It was not so safe outside, as three of the men students found when they crept out and went crouching through the pines to see if the girls in their bungalows were unharmed. A sudden rain of bullets tore through the trees, ripping through leaves and splintering branches, and the men flung themselves to the ground. They had drawn the fire of some Nationalists or Communists – or both? An hour passed before the sporadic shooting died down, and they cautiously continued their journey.

By this time the verandah that had formerly been taken

over by the Nationalists for their machine-gun was recognised by the Communists as a good vantage point, so they set up their own. Again showers of bullets went pouring out, as the machine-gun was whirled round to spray the paddy fields when any movement was spotted there. But after a while they, too, took off their gun and departed, and at last the hillside was quiet again.

The next surprise was the unexpected return of groups of Communist soldiers, marching back along the path they had come, down into the valley. This was not, as Miriam at first thought, an indication that they were retreating. 'They're going back to eat rice,' the servants explained. The Nationalists were presumably likewise engaged, having disappeared in the direction of their headquarters on the other side of the hill. The sun was high in the heavens by this time, and it was time for dinner.

This prosaic explanation of the silence of the guns came like an anti-climax to the alarms and tensions of the morning. 'Time for dinner! Well, everybody's got to eat, even if there is a war on. Maybe we'd better have ours, too!' So it came about that Marvin and Mr. Wang, returning from a moderately successful morning of searching for silver dollars, plodded slowly up the long pathway from the ferry in surprisingly peaceful conditions. As they mounted higher and higher, however, it occurred to them that the silence was ominous. Why were there no people about, no vegetable carriers, no women in the little fields? Had something happened?

Then they saw something that made them catch their breath and gasp – 'Look! What's that? Is it . . .?' It was the dead body of a soldier, lying face downwards near the roadside. Then they saw another – and another.

There was no need for further words. Anxiety lent speed to their feet, and panting they hurried on, fearful of what they would find over the ridge, among the bungalows on the hillside. The tide of war had passed over, and what had it left in its train? As they rounded the last bend, and made their way through the trees towards his bungalow, Marvin saw the door on the verandah open and Miriam step out, to run towards him with outstretched arms.

'Oh, darling,' she gasped. 'Are you all right? I've been so worried about you ... I was afraid you wouldn't be able to get back!'

* * *

For three women missionaries in a walled city in another part of Szechwan the changeover was even more alarming. Their compound was in the direct line of fire between rifle shots from the defenders within and shells from the attackers without. All day they crouched inside their house until towards evening silence fell suddenly, followed by the stentorian voice of the town crier, calling on everyone to come and welcome 'the liberators.' The battle was over. From their balcony they saw files of Nationalist soldiers running out of the west gate, which the Communists had conveniently left uncovered, thus providing a way of escape. As if by mutual consent the two armies avoided confrontations inside towns.

So the wave of war rolled on, with the long, long columns of marching men whose flags were red moving steadily forward. By the end of the year it was virtually over. The Nationalists retreated across the Straits of Formosa, to the island of Taiwan, and the country was left indisputably in the control of the Communists. Communications were restored, the floundering economy began to recover, and Mao Tse Tung was acclaimed far and wide as the Saviour of the People.

* * *

When the C.I.M. leaders in Shanghai came to the united decision that the Mission should remain on in China under a Communist Government, there was much discussion as to how it should be done, what policies should be adopted.

One suggestion made was that missionaries should not be left in isolated places, but should be gathered together in groups in a central town, working out from there. In this way they would be of mutual support in times of difficulty and danger. The idea showed a sensitive perception of the added strain that loneliness can impose in times of tension, but after due consideration it was not adopted. To withdraw from the smaller places would leave the believers there at the very time they most needed encouragement. When it came to priorities, the Chinese Christians must come first.

The political changeover, therefore, found the Mission as widely scattered as ever, with more of its members in twos and threes in outlying areas than were to be found congregated in larger groups in the great cities.

The pattern of events in all places took a similar form. The Communist soldiers behaved extremely well, paying cash for what they bought, frequently giving a helping hand to labourers, and assuring everyone that things would go on just as usual, including freedom of worship. The Buddhists could go to their temples, the Muslims to their mosques, the Christians, where there were any, could go to their chapels, the mysticism of Lao-Tze or the ethics of Confucius could be practised at will – in fact, religious liberty was included in every other liberty now to be enjoyed. A new element of general happiness was introduced by entertainments in the streets, soldiers appearing in some places dressed in long flowing gowns as they walked about on stilts to the admiration and amusement of all who liked that sort of thing. Rousing songs of the revolution, along with an animated form of dancing accompanied by scarf-waving, immediately took on with the young, who proved ready pupils, responding eagerly to the attention now being paid to them.

'What have we to be afraid of?' some of the people asked. 'This regime is much better than the old one!'

When the civic authorities took over, things began to

look more ominous. The political meetings that were held urged the poor to demand their rights – to bring the rich landowners who had exploited them to justice – to voice their complaints against the officials who had deceived them – to expose the supporters of the imperialistic Generalissimo and his Government, now overthrown, and let the people decide their punishment. The voice of the people! Let the voice of the people be heard!

So the accusation meetings began. The wealthy land-lords, the prominent officials, the people who had business interests abroad, must all be brought to trial. Platforms were erected in public places, and the prisoners, roped or chained, were made to stand or kneel before their accusers, and the people called upon to pass judgment.

Confiscate his property! Send him to labour camp! Execute him! Execute him!

Attendance by spectators at the public executions were always viewed favourably, as being a mark of approval. Sometimes it was compulsory, and teachers were instructed to bring their scholars to witness the ceremony ...

House-searching, usually at night, became a common-place. Suspects were taken off for interrogation. In some ways the interrogations were the worst punishment of all, because after hours and hours of it the mind couldn't stop, even when the interrogators ceased their questioning and their probing – it just continued to go round and round, battered into believing its own guilt.

However, people did not talk much about these things. Outwardly life went on much as before, buying and selling, planting and reaping, marrying and giving in marriage. Few rebelled, or resisted the arrests, and those who tried to remain silent at accusation meetings soon learned to put on a show of indignation, and be ready with a denunciation of some sort. The more enthusiastic one appeared to be in favour of the new regime, the less likely one was to attract the attention of the authorities, whose informers might be one's former employees, one's neighbours, one's relatives, even one's children.

It was safer not to trust anyone. In fact, it was safer not even to trust oneself, not to allow oneself to think of any thing except approval of the party line. If one harboured any other ideas, anything that ran counter to the political propaganda sounded out over public address systems in the streets, and at the indoctrination meetings held evening by evening, one might inadvertently betray oneself. Better not to think, better to learn the slogans, repeat them over and over, crushing down the questions that arose in the mind and the inborn instincts of family loyalty.

It did not happen overnight, of course. In the great cities things moved more slowly, or at any rate less openly than in the smaller places, and even there the pressure on foreign missionaries came gradually. In the early days of the changeover, preaching continued with a fervour that was heightened by the uncertainty and apprehension that pervaded the atmosphere, and from all quarters came reports of conversions to faith in Jesus Christ as Lord, and of baptisms sometimes even performed with Communist soldiers looking on.

The impartiality of the western missionaries was demonstrated quite unselfconsciously as they tended the wounded on both sides when need arose. (In some cases the men had been on the march for so long without an opportunity even to change their clothes that they were alive with lice, adding considerably to the difficulty of nursing them.) At first they were more or less ignored by the new authorities, who had other matters to attend to, and other people to deal with. Apart from being told they must register, and that if they wanted to travel outside their districts they would require a permit to do so, they were left to carry on as before, and no restrictions were placed on them.

'Obey the law and you will be free to teach your religion,' said the Communist cadre who came to visit W. A.

Saunders and his wife in their home in south Kansu. On the strength of that assurance Saunders continued visiting the various groups of Christians scattered about the area, encountering no opposition. One day, about a couple of months after the peaceful occupation of the city, however, a leading church elder came to visit him. He had come for a very serious conversation, and it was with obvious reluctance that he came to the point.

'The time has come for you missionaries to leave,' was the gist of what he said. 'If you don't go soon, you'll be in trouble.'

'But why? I was told : . . I've travelled about and no-one has questioned me . . .'

'It may seem all right now, but they're suspicious. The Communists are always suspicious of foreigners, especially those from the U.S.A. and the West. You're from the imperialist nations, remember! You can't avoid getting into trouble.

'And there's another thing. Your Mission has made its mistakes in the past up here in the north-west . . .'

Saunders nodded ruefully. Who hasn't made mistakes, anyhow?

'The past will all be exposed, old grievances aired, and it will go against you, even though you had nothing to do with it personally. I'm warning you. You ought to go.'

A few weeks later Saunders received another warning, this time in church. The young pastor, a gifted local man, was preaching and his sermon was on the prophet Jonah who boarded a ship going in the opposite direction to the one God had indicated. The storm that arose, threatening everyone on board, was entirely due to Jonah's presence on that ship.

'Jonah had to go! Though the sailors were loathe to throw him overboard, the sea did not get calm till they did so!' The inference was clear. The presence of missionaries would endanger everyone in the church when the Communists turned their attention in that direction.

The pastor did not stop at Jonah. There was another storm at sea on his mind, this time the one in which Paul the apostle was involved. Because 'the south wind blew softly' the master of the ship insisted on forging ahead in spite of the apostle's warnings. Then, when a tempestuous wind arose, it was too late. Again Saunders was not allowed to miss the point. The present Communist policy is like the south wind – but beware . . . !

Saunders wrote to Shanghai, reporting what had been said. 'The church leaders would like us to leave, before the trouble starts. They've as good as told us so. They know we'll be an embarrassment to them—foreigners, from the "imperialistic" West . . .'

But about the time his letters were reaching Head-quarters there was a turn of events on the international scene that seemed to promise well for the future.

Great Britain recognized Communist China.

Whatever may have been the private views of British people in China on this action of their Government, it held out greater hope that they would be allowed to remain on in the country. The Government in Peking was not likely deliberately to antagonise a country that was show-ing itself friendly, by oppressing its nationals. It was an encouraging sign.

Besides – China would not change! This was an argu-ment constantly brought forward among the men on Headquarters staff. Down through the millenia the country had survived invasions and political upheavals and remained basically the same. She did not resist her con-querors – she absorbed them! Just wait long enough, and the same thing will happen again. The patience, the wisdom, the power of long endurance that has always characterised the Chinese will outlive Communism and any other ism! They appear to yield, but they always end up by doing things their own way!

So the general advice from C.I.M. Headquarters to its scattered members remained the same. Settle down, continue work and evangelism, obey all regulations that do not go against the conscience. There will be difficulties at first, but we believe if we can stick it out there will be a place for us, as missionaries, in the New China.

Saunders, torn between his conviction that the Chinese leaders were right and that missionaries ought to leave, and his loyalty to the Mission into which he had no doubt God had called him, remained on, continuing his journeys into the country areas until one day he was arrested and taken back to his home under police escort. What worried him most was that the old Chinese Christian who had accompanied him had a bad time of it.

The south wind had stopped blowing softly.

CHAPTER THREE

Year of Crisis

LESLIE LYALL edged his way as quickly as he could through the grave-faced crowd that was emerging from the hall where the meeting had been held and went to find his bicycle. He wanted to get away, back to the quiet compound on Sinza Road, and tell J.R.S. all about it. There was no-one else he wanted to talk to just now. He had caught David Adeney's eye once or twice during the course of the meeting, and knew what he was thinking. No need to stop and talk to him – it was J.R.S. who must know what had been said.

He found his bike, disentangled it from the others piled together against the wall, pushed off from the kerb and sped away through the crowded streets of Shanghai, dodging the bicycles and trishaws, cars and trams that still thronged the thoroughfares. The animated scene with its twinkling lights, its softly gleaming illuminated trade signs hanging outside shops and restaurants, its street vendors with their charcoal fires and stalls of freshly cooked foodstuffs, failed to attract him this evening. Usually he enjoyed cruising along in a leisurely way, savouring the sights and sounds and smells of this cosmopolitan Chinese port. If it lacked the dignity and the beauty of old Peking it had its own clamorous charm at which he smiled tolerantly as he passed between the fairyland of neon lighting along the Nanking Road. It was all part of China.

Tonight, however, he had no thought for it. Impatiently he navigated his bike through the jostling traffic into the quieter streets leading to Sinza Road and through the great iron gates that led into the C.I.M. compound. He put his bike in the shed, unlocked the front door to the staff flats and bounded up the stone stairs to knock briskly on the Sintons' door.

J.R.S. himself opened it. He was evidently ready for bed, for he was in his dressing gown, but he stepped back as soon as he saw who was standing there.

'Come in, Leslie,' he said. 'Sit down. Like a cold drink?' He was back in a minute with a glass in his hand. 'How did it go?'

He'd been wondering all the evening what was happening at the Y.M.C.A. The meeting, at which the four Church leaders who had been called to Peking to see Premier Chou En-Lai were to report on the discussions they had had with him, was to have been attended by a representative group of Chinese Christian leaders and missionaries. They had been bidden in a manner which was more a summons than an invitation and J.R.S. was apprehensive. He'd had a deep sense of misgiving ever since it was known the leaders of the Y.M.C.A., the Church of Christ in China and the National Christian Council had gone to Peking. Something was brewing. 'We may well be facing the darkest period in the history of the Mission in China,' he had said when writing to Arnold Lea in Chungking. Now he was to hear the facts of the case.

'How did it go?' he asked again, and Leslie told him, grimly.

'They want us out – the Government, I mean. The men were told that any troubles the Christians might now be experiencing were due to their being associated with missionaries from the West. It was up to the Church to see they got out of China. Christians ought to be aware that they were being used as a tool by the missionaries who were agents of their governments.

'So they're going to produce what they call a Church Manifesto,' Leslie went on. 'They're going to get every church-goer to sign it. They've got what they call a Three-

Self policy, too! They appointed a committee to see to the wording of it, but in effect what it will say is that the Church promises to make the People's Government its first loyalty, to give unquestioning obedience to the Communist Party, and to purge itself of all traces of Imperialism. And that means us! Purge itself, mind you! The Government isn't going to do it. The Church has got to do it. They've got to get rid of us.'

'So that's it,' breathed J.R.S. 'Whew! The balloon's gone up!'

He saw the subtlety of it immediately. Sign the Manifesto, put your name to something that merely expresses allegiance to the Government of the country, that makes no demand to renounce your faith. Why not? It has nothing to do with God and religion! Many simple-hearted Christians who would face a firing squad rather than deny Christ would sign it without question. And those who perceived what lay behind it, and what it would lead them to do, would be exposing themselves to the hostility of the authorities if they refused.

'Many of the Christians I know won't sign it!' said Leslie stoutly. He thought of the hundreds of ardent young students he had known in Peking, and now in Shanghai, fellows and girls whose Christian faith had already shown itself strong enough to withstand ridicule and deliberate persecution. He had heard them praying together far into the night, their voices rising and falling like waves on the shore, knew the renunciations some of them had made for the sake of the Gospel. 'The I.V.F. leaders won't, I'm sure. And I can't see men like Wang Ming Tao and David Yang pledging their first loyalty to the People's Government, or any other government!'

J.R.S. nodded. He knew them, too. He could not foresee the lengths to which they would go to affirm their faith and manifest their discipleship, the suffering they would endure rather than deny their Master. He could only dimly apprehend it from afar, and it solemnised him. But he was seeing beyond the strong spiritual shepherds of the flocks to the little groups that gathered in small whitewashed chapels, the country Christians who walked miles every Sunday to attend worship, the peasants who could scarcely read the Bibles they treasured so carefully. How would it go with them when they were invited to append their signatures or marks to the Manifesto which apparently only required them to be good citizens in a Communist country? And how would it go with them when it became evident that good citizenship implied foregoing Sunday worship and applying their minds to Communist indoctrination instead, attending public meetings at which their own pastors and church leaders were in the dock, shouting accusations against them, calling for punishment, imprisonment, death?

As for the clause about eliminating all traces of imperialism, in one way this affected J.R.S. even more deeply because it struck at his personal responsibility. The charge of imperialism was constantly being levelled against the western nations and everyone connected with them, and that included missionaries. The Y.M.C.A. meeting had left no-one present in any doubt as to what was intended. 'While China is putting its house in order it is undesirable for guests to be present,' Premier Chou En-Lai had been reported as saying, and the inference was clear. The menacing roar of voices at the accusation meetings, the rifle shots at dawn, the elimination of the wealthy landowners, the truckloads of people being taken to labour-camps told its own story of the way China was putting its house in order. The fewer 'guests' from overseas there were to witness it, the better. J.R.S. thought of the members of the C.I.M. scattered across the breadth of China, who had been instructed to stay at their posts. A few had asserted there would be no opportunity for them to work for Christ under a Communist government and had resigned from the Mission, but the vast majority were remaining on. How would things go for them once the

Manifesto was signed and published? Could the Mission stay on, even in the face of that?

J.R.S. looked across at the younger man and said sombrely:

'This is the beginning of the end.'

But it was only the beginning. The Manifesto had yet to gain the co-operation of prominent church leaders to launch it, and this proved none too easy. A number of those whose names were widely known refused to support it, and the wording had to be written and re-written. Not until mid-September was the full text released to the secular Press, to be published in all the daily newspapers throughout China.

By that time the leaders of the C.I.M. had come to the conclusion that the Mission would still be in a position to continue in China, even in the face of it. Analysing it carefully, they felt that the clause in the Manifesto relating to 'imperialistic influences' did not apply to the Mission. As was explained in the private periodical sent to all missionaries on the field,

'It (the Manifesto) stated that those churches that were depending on foreign personnel or foreign money should make concrete plans for the complete elimination of all such at an early date. Since the churches associated with C.I.M. were already to all intents and purposes independent on both counts, we did not feel the new orders affected us intimately. We would stay on as a Mission as long as God permitted . . . It was agreed at the same time that there might be those of our number who had a personal conviction that the Lord would have them retire from the field.'

It had been made clear, however, that the Mission was definitely not considering opening work in other parts of Asia. Resignation from missionary work in China would be tantamount to resignation from the Mission, unless there happened to be some vacancy on the home staff that would provide the opportunity for further service in it.

One couple resigned, reluctantly. They were new missionaries who had been held up inactive in Shanghai since they arrived in China at the end of 1948, and in the full vigour of their youth believed that God had work for them to do elsewhere. Others in the same group, perplexed, unsettled, nevertheless decided to stay on. God had led them to China in the fellowship of the C.I.M. Of this they had all been certain, so in China they would remain until He showed them another way.

. . . Or until He showed their leaders another way. They had joined a Mission which accepted Director rule, and were prepared to believe their guidance would come through their leaders. They had confidence in their leaders, particularly J.R.S. whom they knew the best, for he was always there, taking his place every day at one of the long tables in the great dining room for the midday meal, attending the morning prayer meetings as naturally and regularly as anyone else, always accessible. The General Director, man of quick sympathy and understanding though he was, was more remote, on doctor's orders, out of the country again. The younger men who were recalled from the provinces, Arnold Lea and Rowland Butler, were still comparative strangers to them. But the sturdy little Scot, second in command, had always been there, imperturbable, unaffected, business-like, addressing God with a quaint intimacy – 'loving Lord' – and they trusted him.

This confidence in J.R.S., widespread throughout the whole Mission, was probably the main factor in holding it together through the increasing tension and uncertainty of that critical year, 1950.

Not that everyone agreed with the policy of remaining on in China, which he upheld. Leonard Street, superintendent of the Mission in the north-west, was getting more and more uneasy about it, and he did not hesitate to say so in his letters to H.Q. Trade-routes from the plains of China, the deserts of Central Asia, the steppes of Inner

Mongolia, converged on the old walled city of Lanchow, where he lived and he knew what was happening in the towns along those roads and on the banks of the Yellow River that flowed down from the mountains of Tibet. The arrests, the interrogations, the accusation meetings, the confiscation of property, the truckloads of political prisoners passing through were creating an atmosphere of fear which was permeating every community. Christian students from the university who were in the habit of attending meetings on the church premises found it hard to sing now, though they had throbbed with joy before. More often than not it was with broken voices they prayed when they were free to come, choking back sobs as they pleaded for the strength they needed to remain faithful to their Lord in the midst of the militant atheism they were encountering.

Political propaganda and Marxist doctrine were the order of the day. 'In the beginning hard work created heaven and earth,' loud speakers blared out across the city, and in the streets a new type of vendor was appearing, as the erst-while well-to-do were reduced to hawking for sale what was left of their belongings after the confiscation of their property, and often enough the imprisonment of the bread-winner.

One missionary, eager to befriend a young woman she saw with an assortment of articles arrayed on a rug spread by the side of the road, was drawn quickly away by her Chinese companion, who whispered, 'Come away! Don't let people see you talking to her. It will make things worse for her ...' For by this time the war had broken out between north and south in the neighbouring country of Korea, and suspicion of westerners had suddenly increased. The reason was not difficult to find. While the People's Government of China was openly favouring the cause of the north, President Truman was ordering U.S. air and sea forces to support the south, and to defend Taiwan into the bargain.

The war in Korea had become headline news through-out China, with America as the prime cause of the conflict. It was secretly reported that in addition to the usual machines of war, the U.S.A. was using a new and sinister method of attack in the form of germs. Germ warfare was even more fearful than poison gas, and who knew where it would spread? People talked about it with bated breath. When it became known that the authorities were suspicious of anyone who referred to it, silence descended on the subject, and if there were those who wondered which side, in fact, was experimenting with this new weapon, they kept quiet about it. Missionaries who laughed at the whole idea, saying they'd never heard of such a thing, were warned to avoid the subject. The authorities would be angry if they knew such things were being said. It was unwise to joke about anything 'they' took seriously. Several missionaries were to learn this the hard way in the days to come.

Meanwhile, the Peace petition was getting under way. This, on the face of it, was innocuous enough. People all over the country were invited to affirm that they were against aggression.

Against aggression? Certainly they were against aggression! They would sign their names to that.

This led on to a concrete case. Were they against aggression in Korea? Yes, they were against aggression any-where.

Being against aggression naturally involved being against the aggressor. That seemed logical.

America was the aggressor! Therefore they were against America?

America was using Christianity to further her own ends—therefore they were against Christianity?

America was using missionaries as agents – therefore they must be against missionaries. Slowly the net was tightening.

In the autumn the 'Hate America – Love China' cam-

paign started in earnest. Enormous posters began to appear
on hoardings with cartoons of P.L.A. soldiers bayonetting
cringing American G.I.s, of infuriated Chinese peasants
rushing against American machine-guns, of Uncle Sam's
hat stuck at a ludicrous angle – on a cross. Demonstrations
were arranged lauding Mao Tse Tung, portraits of whom,
ten times normal size, were carried around the streets
attended by dancing, singing youngsters who intermit-
tently shouted fierce, anti-American slogans.

One such demonstration was planned in the city of
Lanchow, to be held from six p.m. to eight p.m., and
Leonard Street told the missionaries living there it might
be just as well if they remained indoors at that time. That
is why none of them got wet like the crowds who had
gathered in the streets, for precisely at six o'clock the clouds
which had been gathering during the afternoon seemed
to burst simultaneously and the rain poured down with a
velocity that was startling. 'This is no ordinary rain,'
murmured the older people, looking up at the sky with
expressions of awe. The occasional sound of adobe buildings crashing to the ground, undermined by the sudden
torrents of water that swept along the alleys, added to the
uncanny atmosphere.

The procession continued its way along the appointed
route, with very few spectators to cheer it on, for two
hours as arranged. Then the rain stopped as suddenly as
it had started. A few people suggested that the Christians'
God had shown His anger, the Muslims that it was Allah,
but most attributed the phenomena to the 'Old Heavenly
Grandfather', the unseen Being they had always been
taught to believe was up there somewhere – the Most
High.

No-one seemed to think that the 'hard work that had
created heaven and earth' was in any way responsible. As
a wise old man observed during a time of drought, looking speculatively towards the sky, 'hard work doesn't send
the rain.'

Such incidents occurred, now and then, in other parts of China. In one place the demonstration in which Roman Catholic nuns were to have been taken out of prison and paraded through the streets was hindered by just such a downpour, so it was postponed to another day. On that day, too, the C.I.M. missionaries who had been praying that the same thing would happen again rejoiced to see the torrents that seemed to gush from the heavens. The nuns never had to face that particular ordeal of exposure on the streets with its likelihood of physical violence, and were later released.

Those who were hoping and praying for a Divine intervention in the political realm that would change the course of events and relieve the pressure on the churches, however, were disappointed. In one centre missionaries set aside four days for prayer, but things went on just the same, and H.Q. at Shanghai were constantly receiving fresh reports of buildings having been requisitioned by local officials, of increasing difficulty in obtaining travel permits, of the atmosphere of fear that was making people afraid to associate with missionaries.

Jack and Pegi Sharman, in the coastal province of Chekiang, saw ninety-five people baptised one day in July, but then the church building was taken over, the Christians had to register, and questioning began. The Sharmans' house was searched repeatedly, always at night, and they were interrogated regularly. They were denied permission to visit their two boys at school in Kuling, notices stating they were Imperialists were stuck on the city walls, they were forbidden to go outside the city, to visit anyone or be visited. Then Jack was taken out to witness an execution. It was that of a young woman they knew quite well, and after the shot rang out and he saw her writhing on the ground, he was marched away. She was left to die, for the shot had not killed her.

They wrote to J.R.S., and he advised them to get permission to leave, and come to Shanghai. Permission was refused. When they left, it must be to leave the country. By this time the threat of outright war between China and the U.S.A. was bringing with it the shadow of imprisonment, and the possibility that once more, as during the Second World War, the children in school in Kuling would be marched off to internment camps. 'Lord, let our boys get out of China before we go!' was Pegi's daily prayer.

This underlying anxiety about the children in Kuling was shared by all parents, but especially by the men who had the responsibility of making decisions. The value of the school to the Mission was incalculable. For many parents the knowledge that their children were in the same country as themselves, could be visited from time to time or come home to them for holidays, was the decisive factor in keeping them on the field. Whether it was right, in view of the uncertain political situation, to keep the children at school in Kuling was a subject that came up time and again in consultations, but without the assurance that God was leading them to make a change they felt unable to make any other plans.

So the days and the weeks of autumn slipped away with more and more letters coming from inland centres telling of the tension, of Christians being arrested and imprisoned, and of the impossibility now of making any spiritual contribution to the life of the churches, since missionaries were being asked not to attend meetings, as it put the rest of the congregation under suspicion.

'It's difficult for you folk there at H.Q. to understand the atmosphere here,' was a comment made in some of the letters, and J.R.S. knew it was true. Whatever might be happening outside—and the spate of suicides told their own story—on the C.I.M. compound in Shanghai things were still comparatively easy. The alarming news reports brought a sense of apprehension, especially to those whose imaginations were active, and there had been some trouble with servants demanding exorbitant severance pay, but the general tenor of life continued as before. No-one had been taken off for the dreaded interrogations, all were free to attend their churches as usual, there was the usual coming and going, the usual animated chatter at the dinner-table, the regular meetings for prayer and worship, with plenty of hearty hymn-singing. Private personal celebrations, like birthdays, still provided a reason for visiting the Willow Tree Restaurant or the Chocolate Box tea-room in the central shopping area. He felt deeply for those living in isolation in faraway places, cut off from all this fellowship, and wrote a general letter to everyone saying that if any felt they should leave and go home, they must be free to do so and still remain members of the Mission. Then he referred to the Mission itself. Inevitably, in the present circumstances, its numbers must diminish, for no new workers were being accepted, and those who went home on normal furloughs would not be able to return. The possibility of its complete liquidation within a few years might have to be faced.

'The thought that the Mission might actually dissolve within a few years certainly goes like a knife-thrust into one's heart,' he read in one of the letters that came in reply. 'But if the Mission has fulfilled the purpose for which God has brought it into being, then let it be dis-solved . . . if it has not, if God's purposes for it have not yet been completely fulfilled, then *no-one can* liquidate it, I believe, either from without or from within.' He liked that letter, and the note on which it ended, 'Thank God for the men and women in the C.I.M. and the fact that I'm one of them!' That was the way he felt, too. Nevertheless, the way things were going, how could it hope to survive? Indeed, the way things were going now, it looked as if its liquidation might be nearer even than he had feared.

Early in December two events brought things to a head.

One was the arrival in Shanghai of a church leader from a neighbouring province. He had come to see the C.I.M. China Director and his colleagues with a specific request. It was painful and embarrassing in the extreme for him to make it, but the pressure on the churches had become too great. The Manifesto had demanded the elimination of all 'imperialistic influences', and the question was being asked, menacingly:

'Why haven't you purged your churches of Imperialists? Why are these missionaries still with you? Why haven't you got rid of them?'

Now the situation had become unendurable. The request the man had come to make was simply,

'Please go.'

Hard on the heels of this request came one from Chungking, away in the west. Pastor Marcus Cheng, principal of the Chungking Theological Seminary, was asking that all missionaries be withdrawn immediately from his staff. J.R.S. drew his breath sharply as he read it. Had things got as bad as that? That anything would be better than the presence of westerners? He knew it would mean leaving that Seminary virtually without a teaching staff, for the faculty was made up almost entirely of C.I.M missionaries. He knew, too, what a blow this would be to the General Director, who had been on terms of close personal friendship with Pastor Cheng. In view of the two requests, coming so close together, and from such people, how could the Mission remain any longer in China?

CHAPTER FOUR

Order to Withdraw

THE CABLE had gone. Cables and letters had been going all the month, it seemed, keeping the General Director up-to-date with the worsening situation, but this one was different. It advised the withdrawal of all missionaries from areas where their presence was making things difficult for the Chinese believers, and that permission had already been granted to 82 missionaries to prepare to leave China. It was signed 'J.R.S.'. Until he received a reply he would take no further action.

The decision to remain in China, made two years before at the momentous H.Q. meeting when the Bishop held his colleagues to the call of God, had received their unanimous approval and support. None of them had regretted it, nor doubted that it had been right to stand alongside their Chinese Christian brothers and to accept the perils of the civil war and the crisis of the change-over. The results had amply justified the decision. From all quarters had come reports of hearts open to spiritual truths, and of unique opportunities to proclaim them.

The situation was different now.

'Our presence is making things worse for the very people we most want to help. The sooner we get out the better!' was the expressed view of all on the H.Q. staff, and J.R.S. waited eagerly for the reply to his cable. It was a relief to him when it came, though Bishop Houghton's reaction was what he had expected. 'Heartily approve suggested policy where necessary.'

Now he could go ahead and set in motion the plans

already made for what was to him the saddest campaign
in all his life in China.

'It is with sorrow of heart that we have reached the
conclusion that we must proceed with a planned withdrawal of our missionaries,' he wrote heavily. 'It will seem
to many that this is the beginning of the end.' It seemed
like that to him, too. The country that he loved and the
Mission that he loved – to leave the one in her distress
and see the dissolution of the other would be desolating
indeed. The best years of his life had been bound up with
them. *We have you in our heart, to live or die with you*',
the apostle Paul had written to the Thessalonians, and
J.R.S. knew how he felt, for that was the way he felt now.
He mourned as he looked into the future. How bleak it
seemed!

Then something even deeper stirred within him and he
shook off his despondency. After all, his loyalty, his
allegiance, was not primarily either to the Church in China
or to the Mission to which he so gladly belonged.

'But if this is God's way for us, why should we sorrow?'
he asked. The Master had a purpose, and also a plan for
its fulfilment. It was not for the servant to question the
way by which it was to be achieved. As for the Mission,
why assume it must come to an end? Perhaps there was yet
a part for it to play in that plan of God's yet unrevealed.
Meanwhile, the cords of comradeship and the security of
membership must be preserved.

'One reason we have in mind in not asking our friends
to resign from the Mission as they leave China now, is
that the sense of fellowship may be preserved.'

Having written the letter he went to speak at the meeting that had been urgently convened in the Mission home.
Little teams of missionaries living in other parts of
Shanghai came hurrying in, those who were staying in the
Mission Home came down the wide staircase from their
rooms, the offices were closed and the H.Q. staff, the
clerks and the stenographers, all of them members of the

C.I.M., crossed the compound to go in through the glass
doors that led into the tiled entrance hall and passed
quietly into the drawing-room.

No-one talked much. Those who knew what J.R.S. had
to say were silent, and those who did not waited in a rather
oppressive stillness until he arrived. Then, quite simply
and with a solemnity he could not disguise, he told
them.

After eighty-five years in China the C.I.M. is to withdraw...

No longer a help to the Chinese Church, but a
hindrance ... an embarrassment ...

In view of the gravity of the situation the General
Director is calling a conference of all the Home Directors.
It will be held in Australia...

No need for panic. The withdrawal will be phased in
an orderly manner...

It will all cost a lot of money. Let us look to the Lord,
Who has always guided and provided. He will not fail us.
Let us pray...

'Loving Lord...'

*   *   *

After that the HQ. staff got down to business. Regional
Directors sent telegrams to the superintendents, then
letters notifying them regarding procedure.

Keep the lines of communication open ... Send out
the weaker ones first, the elderly, the highly-strung, those
due for furlough. Bring in immediately to the central
station those in the far off remote areas, like the Rupert
Clarke medical team in Hwalung, the Mathews in Hwangyuan, the tribal workers in the south-west...

'What a mercy Isobel Kuhn escaped over the Burma
border! John won't have to worry about her – he'll have
plenty to do, arranging for the others ...!'

The Kuling school – it must have priority. Get the
children out as soon as possible...

The hospitals. Instruct the medical superintendents to hand them over without delay to a responsible body – preferably a Regional Christian Council, as in the case of Kaifeng, but otherwise to the local authorities . . .

Those in difficult circumstances, like the Sharmans, who hadn't been able to get permission to come to Shanghai . . . If they applied for exit visas they might get out! (But the Sharmans were already on their way out a telegram informed them. On the morning of 12 December they had been told peremptorily they were to be deported, and must leave the next day. Unknown to them, at the same time as they got this order a suitable escort had arrived in Kuling and the Principal of the school decided to take advantage of the opportunity to send out four of the boys, including the two Sharmans, to Hongkong.)

Hongkong! Everyone would be converging there, whether they went via Tientsin or Canton! Hundreds of them. Where would they stay? The Colony was already overcrowded, but there was no alternative. 'Cable Kenneth Price to get ready to receive them.'

So the plans were laid, and the matter of money came up, of what it would cost in travelling expenses alone to bring the whole Mission out of China. Suddenly J.R.S. looked across at the man who had remained silent so far during the discussion, and asked with quiet formality:

'Mr. Treasurer, how much is there on the furlough account?'

Frederick E. Keeble, usually addressed as Fred, had been waiting for this question. Finance was his line. The Mission accounts were a source of never-ending wonder to him as he saw them balancing, quarter by quarter, so that however improbable it appeared at times, the Mission never ran into debt. Personal remittances account, station accounts, properties account, special projects account, hospitals account, Kuling school account, he knew them all, and had all the balances up-to-date, carefully tabulated in his mind, ready to be brought out when required. He knew what was expected of him now, and without any delay he replied:

'There is approximately ten thousand dollars on the furlough account.' The furlough account was the one into which a proportion of Mission income was set aside quarterly to provide for the travelling expenses of those due for furlough.

'That would be sufficient for about twenty people,' he added. The silence that followed assured him that the information was sinking in. There was enough money in hand to bring twenty people out of China and back to their homelands, and here they were making plans to evacuate over six hundred, and a couple of hundred children as well!

It was the sort of situation that stirred him deeply. He knew they had no alternative but to go forward, and he had no doubt it was the right course to take. Furthermore, he knew it would be all right. The money would come. If the money did not come, then by some other means the Mission would be brought out of China. God would do it. There was no question in Fred's mind about that. He had been in the finance department for twenty years, and it had left him with no difficulty at all in believing the Biblical records of the widow's cruse of oil that did not run dry, the ravens who brought food to Elijah, the feeding of the five thousand, and the money to pay the taxes, that Peter found in the fish's mouth. The present circumstances were presenting the biggest crisis financially, as well as in other ways, that the Mission had ever faced, but he knew exactly what he would do as soon as this H.Q. meeting was over. He would go straight into Harry Gould's room, and say, 'Harry, write a letter to every member in China, telling them the Mission will meet all expenses to Hongkong, including a hundred pounds weight of luggage for each person, and fifty pounds for each child.' As Financial Secretary it was up to him to make things clear to everyone, and he was ready to take the responsibility, even though the money was not in hand. He knew it would be there when it was needed.

Fred Keeble, however, had a strong sense of the dramatic, and he believed in facing facts.

'. . . sufficient for about twenty people,' he said.

J.R.S. broke the brief silence. 'We must go ahead and trust the Lord,' he said and they all nodded. They had done it before, many times, though never perhaps to such an extent as this. 'We've got to step out in faith. We know we must withdraw.'

Circumstances had forced them to it more than anything in the nature of a divine revelation. In the past there had been occasions when a devotional message of special significance had pointed the way. Sometimes something had happened beforehand to prepare for an unexpected crisis, as when an extra gift of sixty thousand U.S. dollars was received just before the war in the East came to an abrupt end, and provided the needs of the hundreds of C.I.M. missionaries and children who were suddenly released from internment camps. In this case, however, apart from one gift of a thousand dollars 'to be used if you are thinking of evacuation' nothing had been received that was out of the ordinary and funds were only at a normal level. Only in retrospect did it become evident that the hidden process of withdrawing workers from China had been going on for a number of years. Had things remained peaceful there would have been nearly twice as many on the field. The Second World War had closed the door to missionaries on furlough who had planned to return and to recruits hoping to go, while missionaries already in the country had been unable to get out. The eventual dropout through ill-health and change of direction had been considerable. Even during the past year the need for medical attention had been a significant factor in granting early furloughs.

'It is interesting to notice how many are having to leave China these days because of ill-health. I wonder if you have thought why the Lord is using these means of thinning our numbers?' wrote someone as early as May. Six months later the trend was continuing. A gift earmarked for passage money for anyone needing to return home for medical reasons evoked the comment, 'These friends have obviously sensed what we have felt so keenly – the number of our workers who of late have had to go home for health reasons. Possibly it is the way the Lord is using to slim down our numbers in view of the situation.'

These incidents had been mere straws in the wind, however, compared with the irresistible force of circumstances that had forced the decision to withdraw.

'We must move our people out without delay – but how we're going to do it, I don't know,' continued J.R.S. 'We'd better meet together for a special time of prayer, to seek the Lord's help.'

So each day, in addition to attending the usual prayer meeting held every morning before the offices opened, the H.Q. staff met privately in J.R.S.'s room, and very soon the word of the Lord came to them. They had all been receiving private reassurances and promises in their personal devotions, but this was different. The word came again and again, from various sources, and with such a note of authority that they were both exultant and awed.

> 'For you shall not go out in haste,
> and you shall not go in flight,
> for the LORD will go before you,
> and the God of Israel will be your
> rearguard.'   Isaiah 52: 12

They had no suspicion at the time how much they were to need that reassurance. It had not occurred to them that once having decided to withdraw all members there would be any difficulty in getting them out of China. The People's Government would be glad to see the back of them! Even allowing for the long distances some would have to travel, and the complications in winding up business matters,

they estimated the whole withdrawal would probably be
completed in three, at the most four, months.

The winding up of business matters was mainly connected with real estate, and in many places the problem was
being solved for them. The authorities simply requisitioned the buildings they wanted. The summer holiday
homes on Kuling hill station had already gone in that way,
and only the school premises remained. In some places
Mission compounds were being occupied by soldiers, with
the missionaries allowed only the use of the rooms they
lived in. Here and there a quick business deal had resulted
in a sale, but in most cases the property was taken over,
along with a demand for the deeds as well.

'And the same thing could happen here,' said the men
on the H.Q. staff gloomily, looking out of the window of
J.R.S.'s office across to the great six-storied Mission home
opposite.

'I hate to think of the dear old place being used as a
Communist Government department,' someone added, but
they all knew how easily it could happen – and how soon.
'And we need the place till the withdrawal is completed.
Let's pray the Lord will keep it for us – and that when we
have to leave, it will be used for the good of the people
somehow. There's always been something special about
this property.'

The property, indeed, had a history with roots going
back as far as 1885, when Hudson Taylor, the founder of
the C.I.M., had called a special prayer meeting to ask the
Lord's provision of a permanent headquarters building in
Shanghai. Renting property was both expensive and
insecure. It so happened that Archibald Orr-Ewing had
just arrived in China so he, as well as God, heard the prayer,
and since he had recently inherited a fortune he had no
hesitation as to how he should use part of it. He promptly
offered to buy the property and give it to the Mission,
only requesting that his name should be kept out of the
matter.

'The Lord has been dealing with me about not letting people know how He uses His money through me,' he explained simply. How it came about that his name eventually leaked out, many years later, is a mystery. Perhaps God, who loves a cheerful giver, and who saw the self-sacrificing life of His servant as an up-country missionary in China, decided he should have a memorial. Whatever the reason, the C.I.M. Shanghai Mission Home survived various vicissitudes, and when the original old building was sold it fetched a price high enough to provide for the erection of the two large buildings, on a plot of land in Sinza Road, which now comprised the H.Q. of the Mission, and provided a haven for a steady flow of missionaries of other societies as well.

'Lord, this place is the one that *You* gave us, and You've preserved for us all through the years,' was the prayer that went up frequently at the close of the year 1950. 'Lord, we are Thy servants. Don't let us be evicted from it to make room for those who deny Thy very existence. Lord, for Thy Name's sake we ask it . . .' There seemed nothing else they could do after that, beyond keeping their eyes and ears open.

Meanwhile, J.R.S. was preparing to leave China. He was already overdue for retirement, but that was not why he was going. He was needed at the Directors' Conference to be held in Australia, when the matter of the future of the Mission would be the chief item on the agenda. Someone must be there to represent the people who were most vitally involved, the bulk of the Mission, the six hundred and more members still in China. Reluctantly the H.Q. staff agreed he was the one to go, though they hated the very thought of being without him. They were men in the prime of life, but to them he was like a father, and they would feel bereft without him.

Well, they'd see he had a good send-off. Somehow, in the midst of all the sending and receiving of telegrams, the clearing out of old papers and documents, the filling in of innumerable forms demanded by the authorities, word was sent to all members of the Mission that a presentation was to be made to J.R.S., and would they like to contribute. And somehow, from Mission centres in small towns and teeming cities, from C.I.M. members whose minds were being daily oppressed by the atmosphere of fear that surrounded them, word came back, 'Debit my personal account for so much, for the presentation to J.R.S. Hats off to J.R.S.!'

It all had to be kept secret from him and his wife, but fortunately two of the young missionaries had elected to get married, and under cover of the arrangements for the wedding reception preparations were made for a farewell party for the Sintons which was calculated to take them by surprise. On the evening planned, large red Chinese lanterns were hung from the ceiling of the Mission Home entrance hall where small tables and chairs were arranged to make it look as near to being a tea-shop in far-away Szechwan as possible. Somewhat bewildered, the guests of honour were ushered into the seats prepared for them, and the evening started in earnest with everyone drinking Chinese tea and nibbling melon seeds, and making as much noise talking as would be heard in any tea-shop. When the place was comfortably untidy, proceedings started in earnest, with solos, an off-stage musical item representing Scottish bagpipes which J.R.S. found profoundly amusing, and a well-produced skit on his life, including his reactions on being set to work on language study on New Year's Day, and receiving word that his first application for furlough was turned down on the grounds that he and his wife were both in good health and had put in so short a term of service – only fourteen years between them.

When the programme was finished, speeches followed, telegrams were read, and the presentations were made, including a cheque and a folder containing the names of all those who had contributed to it. J.R.S. looked at it, then silently handed it to his wife. So much! They couldn't afford it! He knew what their remittances had been – exactly the same as his own. It was too much . . .

He was conscious of his wife rising to her feet beside him and felt relieved. She could do it better than he could, and there would not be much need for him to say anything by the time she had finished.

'I don't know what to say – how to thank you enough, all of you . . .' she spoke rather tremulously. 'Surely goodness and mercy have followed me all the days of my life.' Then she sat down.

J.R.S. took a deep breath and got up rather slowly. It was obvious that he was unprepared: as surprised as everyone else at the shortness of the speech.

'I thought my wife was going to say something,' he said lamely, and there was a burst of laughter as he continued, 'She doesn't usually have any difficulty in expressing herself!' His loquacious partner chuckled with everyone else at that, and J.R.S. took advantage of the broken sense of tension to get a grip on himself.

'You know, I think you are all very unkind,' he went on. 'Giving us such a send-off—and such a gift. I don't know what to say. It's more than flesh and blood can stand. I never thought of anything like this. I haven't done anything to deserve it. It's been all of you, your loyalty, the way you've backed me up . . .' He was seeing them all in his mind's eye, scattered all over China, the old ones and the young ones, the stolid ones and the impulsive ones, the terse ones and the long-winded ones, the men and women of the C.I.M. who were bound together by the common conviction that God had called them into it, and who had so remarkably, so unquestioningly accepted him, acknowledged his leadership and who were now so unanimously showing him they loved him.

'I can't tell you what it's meant, knowing I could rely on you . . .

'When I came to China I expected to spend the rest of

my life in colportage work, going round the villages selling
Scriptures and preaching a bit. I never thought of anything
else. And now – this! It's too much. It's more than flesh
and blood can stand!'

But for the timely arrival of huge dishes of steaming
meat dumplings and crisply fried spring rolls, creating a
diversion, it might have proved more than flesh and blood
could stand for others that evening.

Especially Arnold Lea. J.R.S. had been like a father
to him from the day he'd stepped off the river steamer, a
gawky youngster uncomfortably conscious of his flapping
Chinese gown, to be greeted by his new senior missionary
with a hearty handshake and the words, 'Welcome to
Chengtu!' They'd got on well right from the start, and
J.R.S. had been Arnold's pattern all along the way up the
line as he'd followed him in the superintendency of the
district, then as Assistant China Director, to the position
he was now to take over as J.R.S. left. Could he ever achieve
that perfect balance, of faith in an all-wise, all-loving God
with genuine sympathy for those who stumbled and fell, in
the way that he had observed in his chief?

That position was going to be even more difficult to fill
than he or anyone else had anticipated. Already the
sanguine expectation that the withdrawal would be completed in three or four months was fading fast as things
took an ominous turn. The People's Government, having
made it impossible for missionaries to stay, was now making
it extremely difficult to leave. No-one could go without an
exit visa, and that was not granted until the applicant could
prove he was leaving behind no unpaid debts. This involved
inserting a notice in the local paper inviting anyone to whom
he owed anything to produce the evidence, so that matters
could be settled. To insert the notice in the paper, however, was not as simple as it sounded. Permission to do so
at all had to be obtained from the authorities, and when
that was withheld there was nothing to do but to wait. No
explanation could be demanded. Already word was coming

of missionaries who were forbidden to go beyond the confines of the city where they lived, and some were under house-arrest.

The most sinister demand made on those wanting to leave the country, however, was that they must have personal guarantors who would stand surety for them even after they left. Each person going out of China was only permitted to do so because a Chinese citizen had promised to be responsible for any unpaid debts, any undisclosed crimes – and for anything the one who left might say or do that was detrimental to the People's Government of China when back in his own homeland. It amounted to leaving a hostage behind, to bear the brunt of any utterance reported that could reflect badly on the Communist Government, and did more to ensure that a blanket of silence covered events in the country than anything else. When someone has risked his own life and liberty to save yours, how can you repay him except by keeping silence if speech will endanger him?

Another problem that was getting more and more acute was the matter of severance pay. Servants had to be dismissed when missionaries were preparing to depart, and suddenly compensation for loss of employment was demanded, and very high compensation at that. In places where servants were being incited or encouraged by the local cadres, exorbitant sums were ordered to be paid, and letters from bewildered missionaries asking what they were to do about it were arriving at H.Q. in increasing numbers. In most cases there was little that could be done but to pay, and it became evident that the cost of the withdrawal from China would be very much higher than had been anticipated. Where would the money come from? Balances on accounts that must now be suspended, like the properties' account and the hospitals' account could be temporarily transferred to the furlough account, but they would soon be swallowed up, and then what?

In normal circumstances it would have been reasonable

to turn the Mission's many assets in the form of property and furnishings into cash, but not much was normal about the present circumstances. It would require little short of a miracle to salvage anything. 'Let's hope we'll be allowed to live in our own premises as long as we're here. That will be something to be thankful for!' was the general attitude now. So when someone on H.Q. staff heard in a round-about way that a hospital committee was on the lookout for premises, and was casting an eye in the direction of the C.I.M. compound in Sinza Road it was with no expectation of receiving any money that Rowland Butler was deputed to make cautious enquiries. If some arrangement could be made with the hospital committee it might safeguard the property from being requisitioned out of hand in the imme-diate future. What was even more important, the place that held such sacred memories would be used for some-thing more in accordance with the purpose for which it had been erected than if it were taken over for Communist government offices or police headquarters.

Rowland Butler set things in motion in an appropriately Oriental manner, and after a few days of mysterious comings and goings announced that the hospital com-mittee was prepared to rent the six-storied Mission Home if it proved suitable for their purpose, to pay three years' rent in advance, and to sign an agreement to that effect.

'Well, how wonderful! Too good to be true, in fact!'

'We shan't get the money, of course, but it will be great if you can get that agreement signed.'

'Go ahead, Rowland! We'll make it a special matter of prayer – the Lord is able.'

So Rowland went ahead and arranged for an inspec-tion of the Mission Home. With its simple architecture and wide entrance hall, its straight corridors and its ele-vators, its huge kitchen and large ground-floor rooms, it was obvious that few alterations would be necessary to turn it into a hospital. The committee expressed itself satis-

fied and a rental agreement was drawn up whereby the
C.I.M. would vacate the premises by nine a.m. on 3 March
1951 when the hospital authorities would take posses-
sion.

'Praise the Lord!' was the heartfelt response to this
news. The first step had been taken. 'Now for the F.A.B.!'

The Foreign Affairs Bureau brooded threateningly on
the horizon of every foreigner in China. From the Foreign
Affairs Bureau they must obtain permission to travel. To
the Foreign Affairs Bureau they must report if they moved
out of the city limits. Applications for permission to
leave the country must be made to the Foreign Affairs
Bureau . . . At one time they had been under the impression they could sell their goods or give them away if they
chose, but by now they had learned they were mistaken.
The Foreign Affairs Bureau must have a say in this also,
and the say was usually 'No.' The 'No' might be a very
long time in coming, however, and in the meantime no
action could be taken.

Rowland Butler wanted to get things moving quickly,
so he prayed for wisdom and applied his mind to the
matter. The wording of his application could be very
significant. To ask permission would merely invite delay.
He submitted it with a note to the effect that the agreement
would be signed on the following day – unless the Foreign
Affairs Bureau forbade it.

As he expected, the F.A.B. promptly refused to give
permission.

'They've refused to give permission, but they haven't
forbidden it,' he pointed out to his colleagues. 'There's a
subtle distinction there. The fact is, they're in a bit of a
quandary. They wouldn't mind forbidding us to sign it,
but it's another matter for them to forbid the hospital
committee to sign it. That committee happens to be under
the authority of the highest military commission in East
China! Even the F.A.B. would hesitate to get up against
that!'

'And that military commission happens to want our premises! You've got something to go on, there! Keep on talking, Rowland, and we'll keep on praying.'

The parleying continued, and after some days the F.A.B. said that *if* the agreement were drawn up and signed a copy of the contract must be sent to them.

The contract was very carefully drawn up, duly signed, and a copy sent to the F.A.B. As soon as they received it they 'phoned to say that on no account were payments to be received from the hospital until their Bureau had ratified the agreement.

Their Bureau did not ratify the agreement. Silence fell.

'Keep on praying, and I'll keep on making enquiries about the status of that agreement,' said Rowland, and after three weeks a terse communication from the F.A.B. stated that in no circumstances could the agreement go through in its present form. Six changes must be made. Only then would the F.A.B. ratify it. From the tone of the communication it was evident that the Bureau was extremely annoyed.

'It's got to do with the rent, that's sure!'

'Paying three years in advance, and still retaining the title deeds! Might have known it would land us in difficulties. Well, we'll have to go and face the music.' So off went Rowland with a colleague to give him moral support, while the others had a special prayer meeting before getting on with their own work.

Hours later the two returned, and went straight in to see Arnold.

'We've seriously offended the People's Government,' they said, 'by the way the agreement was drawn up. There were several things they objected to, but one in particular they said was an affront to the people of China. We were duly penitent, of course, assured them that no affront had been intended, and asked to be told what it was, so that we could put it right. You'll never guess what it was.' They could keep their faces straight no longer, and grinned widely as they explained. 'It was the clause about the drains.'

'The drains!'

'Yes. The drains. There's a clause to the effect that those renting the property must be responsible for keeping the plumbing in good working order. It's normal procedure to include it in such documents. But the F.A.B. were highly incensed. We didn't enquire whether the fault lay in mentioning the drains at all, or whether it lay in suggesting the People's Government wouldn't look after them properly. It was as much as we could do to keep from bursting out laughing or sighing with relief, but we knew enough to keep our faces solemn, and apologise profusely. Of course, we said we would delete the clause altogether. The other points they raised were equally unimportant.'

'No argument about the price? Rent in advance? Retaining the title deeds?'

'None at all. The only stipulation is that the money can't be taken out of China. It must all be used inside the country. If we get the money at all, that is,' Rowland added cautiously. It still remained to be seen if the military commission would honour the agreement.

The military commission honoured the agreement. The first instalment was paid into the Mission's account a few days later, according to arrangement, and it was evident the rest would follow. (Not only did they pay the money in full, but also bought a lot of the furniture, and eventually took over the office building as well, paying six months' rent in advance for it.)

When Fred Keeble entered the money on the Withdrawal Account, he spent a lot of time working on some figures he had before him which had to do with the cost of railway travel, river boat travel, bus travel, every form of travel from various places in China down to the border between Canton and Hongkong. Then he turned, frowning, to another set of figures and scribbled again on his pad. After a time he pushed them all back, gave a deep sigh, and looked across the desk to where Harry Gould was sitting.

'Harry,' he said, and his face was aglow. 'The Lord's done it again – just like that, in one sweep!' All his life long he'd never get over the wonder of it, the way God met the needs. 'I've been reckoning it all up, and I believe the money from the rent of that dear old building is going to pay the whole cost of the withdrawal from China – severance pay and all!'

CHAPTER FIVE

Rainbow in the Cloud

THE ONLY C.I.M. field centre outside China was a three-bedroomed twin flat in a tall building on the waterfront in the Crown Colony of Hongkong. Here lived Kenneth and Vera Price with Bob and Muriel Ament and their three children, and since the Prices had their hands full with financial affairs, it worked very well to live together as one family with Muriel doing the housekeeping. There wasn't room with such accommodation to put up the straggling stream of missionaries who crossed the border from time to time, en route for furlough, but a small Chinese guest house nearby, run by Christians, took them in. None of the transients stayed long, for it was part of Bob Ament's job to ensure that they got away, by sea or air, at the earliest possible moment. Living expenses in Hongkong were higher than anywhere else in the Far East, and the C.I.M. encouraged its members to use it merely as a stepping stone, not a resting place. Visits to shipping offices to pick up a tourist-class booking here, another one there, was part of his job as business manager for the Mission in Hongkong. Wealthy Chinese refugees were flocking into the Colony and clamouring for ways to get out to the west. Hongkong was a bottleneck, and accommodation so hard to find that people were sleeping in the streets, in doorways, and even on staircases.

When, therefore, the cable arrived with its cryptic information that the Mission was withdrawing from China, followed by instructions 'Prepare to receive them', the Prices and the Aments looked at each other open-eyed and open-mouthed. They were speechless for a few moments, and when they found their tongues their verbal reactions were thoroughly human.

'Receive the whole Mission - over six hundred people!'

'Not to mention the children from Kuling!'

'And all their baggage!'

'Where on earth can we put them? If we clear out the offices, and all sleep on all the floors we couldn't accommodate more than about twenty ... And then there's the food to get ...'

'Has everyone at H.Q. gone mad? Don't they know it's impossible to rent even a room here without paying an exorbitant sum in 'key money' first, on top of the rent?'

'Talking of money,' said Ken Price, the accountant, drily, 'they didn't mention it. I haven't any idea what money we can spend. They've got all the accounts in Shanghai.'

'It'll take thousands, tens of thousands of dollars to get passages for them all to ship them home – and where am I going to get those passages, anyway?' Bob Ament remembered the long, long lists at the shipping offices, and groaned. 'As for what it will cost to keep them all here ...!

'It'll need a miracle!' Something within them began to stir, to rise to the surface, and they sat back more quietly. 'Only the Lord can do it. We'll have to trust Him. He'll do something. After all, it's His work, and we're His servants. He's sure to have a plan. Let's pray ...'

So faith took control again. Their Master had promised that those who put the affairs of His Kingdom first, and conducted their lives according to His standards of rightness, would be provided with what they needed. For years they had lived on that principle and had found that it worked, in spite of their mistakes. It was, after all, the principle on which the whole Mission had been founded and had continued until now. They had never been confronted with anything of this magnitude before, but their experience of Hongkong told them what to do along practical lines.

Type lists of all C.I.M. personnel for the police and immigration authorities.

Guarantee all will pass on with the minimum of delay. 'No problem there. They all hold bona fide passports to their home countries – unlike these thousands of Chinese refugees flooding in, penniless, stateless, unable to go any farther!'

Reserve as many tourist-class passages as possible to Australia, New Zealand, Britain, Canada, the States, South Africa . . . anywhere, to get people moving out. Call the shipping offices daily in the hope of a cancellation.

Freight and cargo vessels take a few passengers – try them.

. . . And find accommodation. This was the most urgent requirement, and the most unobtainable. Visits to real estate agents, to hotels, to boarding houses, to schools, to churches, anywhere likely to have empty rooms, halls, dormitories, all drew a blank. Even the very high Government official who was approached expressed his sympathy and concern, but could do nothing. The Colony had more than doubled its population in less than two years, and all available space was already being utilised. Chinese refugees were living on the hillsides in shanties they had erected themselves out of cardboard, tin, wood, sacking, anything they could find. Where were six hundred missionaries and a couple of hundred children to be housed? There seemed no answer.

The search continued, and the influx started. Little groups of missionaries in twos and threes came over the border, were accommodated somehow, and sent on their way.

'We might be able to manage if they came slowly, but what's to happen when the big parties arrive?' asked the Aments.

Then came the news that the Kuling school was to be evacuated as soon as possible, and that the first contingent of children with their escort would be arriving in a week's time. The others would be following almost immediately.

The situation was so impossible that they looked at each other and laughed. God must be going to do something now! They went on praying and they went on searching, but they found themselves strangely care-free. Faith had that effect. Somewhere in the overcrowded Colony, either on the Island, in Kowloon, in the New Territories, somewhere God had accommodation waiting for them. If they went on seeking they would surely find it, even if it were miles away.

It was not miles away, however, but nearer and more conveniently situated than anything they had so much as wistfully thought of, though they came across it in a very circuitous way, and nearly missed it altogether.

Bob Ament, making his rounds of the estate offices, arrived in one on the Island, where he had already been so recently he was almost ashamed to turn up again. He slumped gratefully into a chair when the estate agent, glancing quickly at him, said kindly:

'Take a seat. You look as though you'd had it. I'm afraid I've got nothing for you,' he continued reluctantly. 'I just can't find anything.' He looked across the desk at his client and, trying to be helpful, thought for a few moments, then added:

'What you want is a dozen quonset huts. You could fit them up and make them quite habitable.'

'Yes, I'd thought of that, too,' replied Ament. 'Even went to the top level to see if I could get any. Not one available . . .'

But the agent was not listening. His own words had arrested him.

Quonset huts. Where had he seen them quite recently? On the waterfront somewhere . . .

'I remember!' he said suddenly. 'I know where there

are some. I saw them a month ago. They're on the Chatham Road in Kowloon.'

Ament subsided limply. 'Listen,' he said, 'I live on the Chatham Road. I know those huts. They're nearly opposite our apartment. They're all occupied by the military.'

'I don't mean those,' the agent replied briskly. 'There's a block of land behind them, by a railway siding, at the back of the crematorium. There are eleven quonset huts there. Government property. They're pretty dilapidated, but they were empty. If they're still vacant and you could get them for a few months ... Why not go and find out?'

Bob Ament shot out of the office, down the crowded street to the quayside, pushed his way on to the ferry-boat, stiff with people, going across the water to Kowloon, darted off as soon as it berthed, swung on to a bus going along the familiar stretch of Chatham Road, and got off at the railway siding. It was just as the agent had described it. On a derelict plot of land, out of sight of the road, behind the crematorium, stood eleven quonset huts. Some of the windows were boarded up, some were broken, doors were missing, they presented a dreary enough sight standing there among piles of rubble and rusty wire – but they were empty!

Back to the ferry went Bob Ament, across to the Island, up to the Government buildings and into the office of the sympathetic, highly placed British official who had told him to keep in touch 'and let me know if you get anything.'

'Eleven empty quonset huts behind the crematorium on the Chatham Road,' explained Ament. 'Government property. If we could be allowed to use them ...'

'I didn't know of these,' said the official. 'Wait while I find out about them.' Ament waited, an urgent prayer in his heart. When the enquiries had been made, the official turned to him and said:

'Now we shall have to go through three government

departments – and I suppose you've heard of red tape?'

'Yes,' was the reply, 'and the first party of school-children is due to arrive in less than a week!'

The two men sat in silence. Red tape. Files, Reports. Restrictions. Agreements. Bye-laws. All that and more on the one hand, and on the other a crowd of British and American 'missionary kids' coming out of Communist China with nowhere so much as to sleep when they got into Hongkong.

The government official knew none of those children personally, but the kinship of nations is very strong, and government departments are manned by human beings. There would be a lot of work to be done behind the scenes, untying that red tape, but . . .

'I'll risk it,' he said. 'I'm so sure we'll get those huts,' and he gave orders that the demolition work was to cease immediately. Then he turned to Ament with a smile and said:

'Go ahead and make them habitable!'

How to set about the task Ament did not know, for the plumbing and the electrical wiring had already been removed, doors and windows needed renewing, walls must be repaired, and the whole site cleared of its rubbish. In addition, beds and bedding would be required for at least a couple of hundred people, and arrangements made for providing meals. He did not know where to start, but he knew someone who would be able to advise him.

How much hinged on that one Christian friend! An architect and an engineer, member of a well-known Hong-kong family, Hugh Braga not only knew exactly what to do, but seemed prepared to divert his entire staff from their normal work to ensure that it was done.

Insufficient wiring and outlets to complete the restoration of plumbing and electricity? He had a quantity of just the right sort of material in hand, which he had previously refused to sell, though it would have fetched a good price. Let it be used now. Deliver it immediately.

Water to be laid on? Get in touch with the Water Department.

Beds and bedding required? See the Social Welfare Officer.

Authority required to erect poles for overhead cables on railroad property? Contact the Manager of Railways.

So it went on. The deserted site became the scene of determined activity as rubble was cleared away, rebuilding took place, electric lights flashed on and water gushed from taps once more. By the time the first group from Kuling arrived, young teenagers clutching their cricket bats and their tennis racquets, their footballs and their violins, the beds were neatly arrayed along each side of the walls in the quonset huts, with plenty of room between them for suitcases and trunks.

'What a haven!' remarked someone. The teachers who had escorted the youngsters looked round approvingly. 'So secluded, and right away from the road.'

'And it's free!'

'In a free country!' added someone else feelingly.

'There you've got its name,' said Ken Price. 'We call it Freehaven.'

* * *

The provision of Freehaven was followed by a set of circumstances, apparently equally incidental, that led to the solution of another quandary. The difficulty of obtaining passages out of Hongkong was greater than ever. Business people were leaving China in large numbers, all eager to return to the west, and travel agencies had nothing to offer but first-class accommodation on liners or seats on planes. Both were too expensive for missionary societies, and the only hope Bob Ament had of moving on the people piling up in Freehaven was if a last-minute cancellation could be taken up at a reduced price. Ones and twos were getting away, but what he needed was to ship them off by the score!

'Lord, we pray Thee to provide us with swift transport out of Hongkong,' was a constant prayer, though no-one could forsee how it could happen. Visits and telephone calls were made to all the travel agencies almost daily, however hopeless the application might seem to be. None of them was left in any doubt as to whether or not the C.I.M. wanted passengers out of Hongkong.

Perhaps it was this persistence that gave the manager of Thomas Cook's Travel Agency an idea when he heard that the Eagle freight planes were returning to London empty after delivering their cargoes in Japan.

'Would you be interested in chartering planes to London?' he enquired, and Bob Ament shook his head.

'We've made enquiries along that line,' he answered. 'Far too expensive for us.'

'But this is different,' explained the manager. 'The Eagle Line is not a passenger one, but carries freight. They might be glad to get a payload for the return journey. Shall we get in touch with the pilot next time one of their planes touches down here? It might be worth trying.'

The outcome of that conversation was that a few days later the pilot of an Eagle Airline plane was asked if there was any possibility of his taking a load of human freight on his return flight, and his response was immediate. Indeed there was! He was delighted. He estimated that he could take up to forty passengers and their baggage on each trip. Returning from Japan to London with an empty plane each time was expensive and bad for business, but all his efforts to find customers had been unavailing. Every door had closed.

'The Lord was keeping it for us,' said the Aments and the Prices to each other afterwards, marvelling at this utterly unlooked for provision. 'He heard our prayers for swift transport – quicker than anything we'd thought of.'

'He bore them on eagles' wings,' said someone, and they all laughed exultantly. If the quotation was taken slightly out of context, it seemed to fit the case. The airline had been very appropriately named. The cost for each passenger was only a fraction more than for tourist-class travel on a liner, and the flights to London started almost at once. As Freehaven filled up with the groups of missionaries who were travelling down through China into Hongkong, so it was emptied again as another Eagle plane took off for England.

It was during one of those flights westward that the passengers were silently yet convincingly reminded of a God who keeps His promises. The plane, having flown in clear skies over Asia, entered clouds as it turned northwards into Europe. The mighty forest-clad mountains of South-East Asia, the plains of India, the deserts of Arabia and the blue waters of the Mediterranean had all been visible, but now there was only mist and billowing cloud. No longer was it possible to watch the changing panorama of earth below by peering out of the windows, and the travellers settled back in their seats to read or chat, when suddenly one of them exclaimed:

'Look at that!' and pointed excitedly out of the window. There in the cloud was a rainbow, clear, vivid yet translucent, travelling alongside them. It was not, as they had sometimes seen on the earth, a perfect arc stretching from horizon to horizon. What arrested their attention to this rainbow was that it was a complete circle. And right in the centre of it, like the apple of an eye, was a shadow. Rather awed, they gazed at it. Encircled by that luminous colourful ring was the little shadow of the plane in which they were travelling. Several times they saw the rainbow as they sped through the clouds that day. Sometimes it was small, clear and distinct, sometimes wide and hazy, the colours dim; but always, in the centre, was the shadow of the plane. It was as though a message from the rainbow-circled Throne itself had reached them,
The Lord thy God is with thee withersoever thou goest.

* * *

The supply of ample withdrawal funds through the renting of the Shanghai property, the provision of Free-haven and then the Eagle flights gave a thrill of encouragement to the whole Mission, outside China as well as in. What provided an even greater incentive to the faith and expectation of its supporters in the homelands, however, was the outcome of the Directors' conference that was held in Australia. Home Directors from North America, Australia, New Zealand, Great Britain and Switzerland met the General Director there in what was certainly the most critical period in the history of the Mission. It was drawing out of China, the country in which its entire missionary activity and experience had been centred, and for which it had surely been brought into being. There had never been any serious consideration given to its working anywhere else. The matter had been raised earlier, but had been put aside. The question that had to be answered now was whether this was the end, whether the time had come for the liquidation of the China Inland Mission.

Over the years various illustrations had been employed to describe the character of a missionary society in a foreign land, and recently the rather mundane and unpicturesque example of scaffolding had been used. The missionary society, it was pointed out, was merely for the purpose of helping in the erection of the Church in the land. It was not intended to become an integral part of it. For a time it might be all that could be seen, but as the hidden building grew the time would come when the scaffolding would be removed altogether. 'Not in haste, nor haphazardly, but with care, that the scaffolding materials may remain for use elsewhere.' Or as in a shipyard, where the props are essential while the boat is being built, but become hindrances when the vessel is ready for launching. Since God was the Master-builder, not man, it was for Him to decide when the props were to be taken away, to be used again in some other place where He had work to be done.

The men who gathered in Kalorama, Australia, spent

two days in prayer before discussions started, but after that soon came to the conclusion that the Mission must continue. Fred Mitchell, Home Director for Great Britain, was vehement and eloquent as he stressed the point that God had not only called men and women to serve full-time in the Mission, but that they were supported by thousands upon thousands of friends and helpers whose prayers and spiritual activities centred in it. It would be a loss to the whole Church if this vast company, with its potential for effective service anywhere, were disbanded. He thought of the little groups who gathered regularly to pray for the Mission and its work, of people who for years had been giving liberally from their incomes to support it, who even now were anxiously awaiting the result of this conference. Was he to go back and tell them it was all over, that the Lord had no further use for the organisation of which they were so vital a part?

And was the task of world evangelisation complete? asked someone else. Were there not vast areas in the Far East alone where there was no witness for Christ, and where the doors stood open?

The Lord had called the C.I.M. to work among the Chinese, volunteered another. There were literally millions of Chinese living outside China, in South-East Asia. Missionaries who spoke Chinese could start reaching them for Christ without delay.

On the third day of the conference it was unanimously agreed that God was directing the Mission to send workers to most of the countries of South-East Asia. It was not clear, however, whether that commission included Japan. The reasons for and against reaching so far north seemed to balance each other, and as the day dawned when some decision must be made, opinions were still flexible.

Then something happened that convinced them. That very day two letters arrived, both containing news of gifts designated for work in Japan. The significance of the timing of those letters was not lost on the members of the conference. God's stewards render a double service when their gifts are sent at the right moment. The outcome of the historic Directors' conference held early in 1951 was that cables were sent to the various headquarters announcing that the Mission would be embarking on evangelist work in Thailand, Malaya, Indonesia, Hongkong, the Philippines – and Japan.

The announcement was greeted with enthusiasm in the homelands, and almost immediately requests for help started coming in from other societies working in South-East Asia. There were urgent needs that people with experience among the Chinese could meet in the areas where they were at work. Missionaries on furlough waited eagerly for further news, and plans were set on foot for experienced men to go to survey the unevangelised areas. In the midst of the darkening picture in China the challenge of open doors and new opportunities elsewhere was stimulating.

In Hongkong the reaction was less favourable. The men and women in Freehaven who had just emerged from China were still oppressed by the tension under which they had lived, and the thought of those they had left behind. 'My heart is still in China,' many of them said. 'I don't feel called to go anywhere else. The only thing for me to do now is to go home.' A few were prepared to turn their thoughts to other lands, but the majority were slow to do so.

As for the response in Shanghai H.Q. to the news, it was cool in the extreme. The arrival of anyone from the interior en route for Hongkong was greeted with general relief, for the authorities were increasingly slow in granting exit visas, and events were taking an ominous turn with accusations being levelled against missionaries, and local believers being taken off for interrogation, imprisonment, in some cases to the execution ground.

Over and above the anxiety over fellow-missionaries in difficulties was the burden of grief for the Chinese

Christians. They must stay on whatever happened, be prepared to endure indefinitely the hostile atmosphere of militant atheism that could lead them to labour camps and prison if they resisted, or to the betrayal of their Lord and His servants if they yielded. Already harrowing stories were seeping through of the suffering some of them were enduring, of days and nights of incessant, piercing interrogation, of the fear that led to invectives against erst-while colleagues, of chapels being closed and the believers scattered. This was what concerned them, not the unevangelised millions of South-East Asia.

Arnold Lea, in the position of responsibility into which circumstances had thrust him, was torn between his loyalty to the Mission and his love for the Chinese. The conflict within was intensified by having to try to keep it to himself, and there were times when he longed to talk things over with J.R.S., to give voice to the emotions deep within him.

'We have to get out of China, but that doesn't mean we have no further responsibility for it. The Chinese Church is facing its Gethsemane. Can we not at least watch with it one hour? It needs our intercession now as never before. This talk about "new fields", this enthusiasm for something fresh will only divert prayer and interest away from those to whom we are bound by the closest spiritual ties, our fellow-labourers in the Gospel, those we have prayed with and worked with and suffered with, many of whom have stood by us so courageously through these past difficult months, and who have suffered the more because we didn't get out earlier!

'How can we turn away so quickly and get all excited about other opportunities when our brethren are enduring torture, physical and mental, and in danger of cracking under the strain? It's for China, for the Chinese Christians that the call to pray ought to be going out incessantly, mobilising all the C.I.M. prayer groups to call mightily upon God for His strengthening, and His deliverance!

That sort of prayer is costly, it demands concentration and persistence in the face of silence, as less and less news gets out of China. But they're depending on us for it. Time and again, as our missionaries get away, the last words that come to them are "Pray for us!"

'Besides – do we really believe this is the end of our work in China? I don't! Nor do many of our Chinese brethren!'

Watchman Nee and some of his colleagues had recently visited the C.I.M. compound in Sinza Road, and expressed the belief that Communism would not take root in China, and that the day would come when missionaries could return. 'What would you want us to do then?' Arnold had asked, and the prompt reply had been, 'Bible teaching. And meanwhile, prepare translations of Bible commentaries, Bible handbooks, the spiritual treasures of the centuries that are available to you in the West. Be ready to share them with us when you come back.' In the light of remarks like that, should the Mission not be poised, ready to return to China when the door opened again? Shouldn't the whole emphasis of the Mission continue to be on China?

If these were his deepest thoughts, and those which he expressed somewhat forcefully in his letters to the Directors out of the country, they had to be buried most of the time, for the very pressure of immediate affairs filled his mind and his days. The clearing out of the Mission archives, the sorting of papers, the tearing up of books and documents called for constant decisions and consultations, for the most innocuous reports could be used as incriminating evidence against any who did not toe the Communist party line. In addition, telegrams and letters were being received all the time from missionaries in the interior, all demanding a reply.

'Sometimes the news we receive from many of you is good,' he wrote in a long letter on 9 March, which was circularised to all C.I.M. centres in China. 'Frequently we go for days without hearing anything encouraging, while at other times the postman or the telegraph boy brings us disquieting tidings.' It had been a very unpleasant thing to receive a telephone message one Saturday afternoon giving the news that Dick and Marian Springer had been taken off to prison. He knew they had had a harassing time for some weeks, being taken off for frequent interrogations, but to have lost their liberty altogether meant that their small children were left in the charge of someone else. What would be the outcome of it all? Sunday was an anxious day for Arnold, acutely conscious that there was nothing he could do to help but by prayer. When a wire was received on Monday morning saying that the whole family was now on the way to Hongkong it was almost unbelievable. The relief was overwhelming.

Deliverances were not usually granted so quickly, however. Nearly four hundred workers were still scattered throughout China, unable to move until they received their exit visas. The withdrawal was not proving so simple as had been anticipated. Arnold looked back to the time, just three months before, when the problems that had loomed largest had been practical ones concerning money and transport, disposal of property and the possible resistance on the part of some missionaries who would want to remain on in China. These problems had all been solved almost before they arose. There was ample money in China from the rent of the H.Q. property, funds were flowing in freely from the home centres for the heavy expenses of conveying missionaries back, there was nothing that could be done about Mission buildings, in most cases, so that at least presented no problem. As for anyone wanting to remain in China, that number was already minimal, for the situation was worsening daily, with the Korean war introducing an intensified anti-American feeling. No Chinese wanted to associate openly with foreigners from the western nations.

The situation that was developing now was more subtle,

even sinister. It was like being involved in a war of nerves. Missionaries here and there were being harassed without explanation, refused permission to start advertising in preparation for applying for an exit visa, visited at night by police who demanded to search the premises, taken off for long periods of questionings and required to fill in forms giving a detailed summary of their movements from birth, and sometimes of their parents before them. Some, complete with exit visas, had been stopped from travelling at the last minute, with no reasons given. Others were being threatened with appearing before a People's Tribunal to face unspecified accusations. The imprisonment of the Springers, brief as it had proved to be, had opened up the ominous possibility that others might be treated in the same way. The probability was that they would not get away so soon.

The whole situation was becoming strangely reminiscent of the position of the Children of Israel when in Egypt, oppressed and hated, yet unable to leave.

The analogy occurred to several people during those early months of 1951, among them Mrs. Mason.

Mrs. Mason was, in a way, unique. In the first place, she was the only member of the Mission who had the advantage of being half-Chinese, so her knowledge of the language, the thought patterns, the culture of the people was inherited, not acquired by hard study and sometimes perplexing experiences. In the second place, she occupied an exceptional position in the Mission compound in Shanghai, because although she lived in the Mission Home, she had no specially assigned tasks like the others at H.Q., who were there either as administrators, or office workers, or as superintendents in the Mission Home. She came and went as she pleased, and the reason for this was that she was unusually gifted as what is known as 'a personal worker'. Her relationship with the Lord was so unaffected and natural that she could speak of Him spontaneously and without bringing a sense of embarrassment, no matter in what company she found herself. She explained sometimes that when her husband had died, leaving her a childless widow, she knew she would be lonely and want someone to take his place. 'Thy Maker is thy husband,' the prophet Isaiah had proclaimed to Israel, and since she was part of the spiritual Israel she could take the promise to herself. She needed a companion and a friend, a protector and a leader in her life, especially now that her husband was with her no longer, so 'I'll take Jesus as my husband,' she had said to herself, and had found Him perfectly satisfying.

There was no wistfulness of widowhood about Mrs. Mason. Plump and smiling, dark eyes twinkling happily, she had innumerable Chinese friends who sent cars or pedicabs to fetch her to their parties and feasts, to which she went immaculately clad in her long, high-necked Chinese gown, a Bible in her handbag. Sometimes they came to see her. One never knew in what corner of the Mission Home, in the drawing-room or in the hall, one might come across a little group of Chinese ladies sitting around Mrs. Mason, listening to her as she explained something from the Bible or joining in as she started them up singing a hymn or a chorus. She did it all quietly and unobtrusively, so that it did not interfere with anything else that might be going on, but she was undeterred by surroundings and circumstances, her main task in life being to 'introduce people to Jesus'.

She was equally uninhibited in the Prayer Hall, where the Mission prayer meetings which everyone attended were held daily. Sometimes the prayer meetings were very solemn occasions, and there were those who felt too over-awed by the atmosphere to break the silence by opening their lips and giving voice to their prayers in public. Not so Mrs. Mason. If she had something on her mind she came out with it. Her clear, warm voice was often the first one to be heard when the leader of the meeting said, 'Now let us pray'.

On one such occasion her mind was very full of the menacing situation which fellow-missionaries in the interior were facing. Like everyone else in the meeting, she was aware that an unseen force was at work, hostile and cruel, hindering their departure, and the familiar records of the Exodus impressed themselves upon her, particularly the steady, insistent command of God Himself when He sent word through Moses again and again to the adamant Pharaoh:

'Let My people go.'

The conflict had been a long and fierce one, but eventually the Enemy had collapsed defeated, and the Children of Israel had made their historic departure from Egypt. In that long record was a little phrase which had somehow fastened itself in Mrs. Mason's memory. 'There shall not a hoof be left behind.'

It spoke of complete deliverance, but in the present circumstances it was not sufficiently specific. It was not horses and cattle that were involved, but human beings, and the threat of some of them being imprisoned was beginning to hang heavily over the meeting. There were already one or two men of other Missions who were in jail in the interior, and who knew when they would be released. Who knew *if* they would be released? Mrs. Mason was deeply moved, urgently pleading for her beloved China Inland Mission, and everyone in it.

'Lord!' she prayed. 'Bring them all out. Everyone. Let not a hoof – nor a husband – be left behind!'

When the meeting was over, and people walked quietly out, they looked at each other and murmured, with affectionate amusement:

'I say! Did you notice Mrs. Mason's prayer?'

'I should say I did! "Not a hoof nor a husband." I *had* to smile!'

But they had to admit that it was very relevant. The women and the children would be sent out first, but some men would have to stay behind to clear up affairs before they could leave themselves. If one here, and one there, were refused permission to go, if they were hauled before a People's Tribunal and sentenced to imprisonment, hard labour, death, who could stop it? In the months and years that followed Mrs. Mason continued praying in the same words:

'Lord – let not a hoof nor a husband be left behind.'

CHAPTER SIX

The Pressure from Within

I'M REALLY ENJOYING myself now!' said Miss Chang as she sipped with relish the rich brown liquid from the cup in her hand. 'I don't know how many years it is since I drank cocoa.' With her clumsy home-spun clothes and large cloth shoes she looked like a peasant from the country, though she spoke with a pure Peking accent and had entered the Mission Home at Shanghai as though quite accustomed to large, city dwellings. She shot a merry yet significant look at her companion and added:

'I wonder what sort of trouble I shall be going back to? Prison again, maybe.' The prospect didn't seem to oppress her or dim the enjoyment of the moment. 'It'll be the ninth time, if so. I'm getting quite used to it,' and she chuckled. 'Not that it's pleasant you know—not like this.' She glanced round the simply furnished bedroom with its plain wooden furniture and its chintz curtains appreciatively. 'Very dirty it can be in prison. Strange company, too!' She wriggled in her clothes as though she was itching, scratched herself, then made a sudden jab with thumb and forefinger at some invisible object and held them aloft triumphantly. 'Got him! A big fat flea! You know the sort?'

Her companion (the writer, as it happened) nodded with a grin. She understood the pantomime. Country work in the villages of inland China had made her well acquainted with that sort of company.

'But when you're cold you can put up with it,' continued Miss Chang. 'It was bitterly cold one time in prison when I was there, and I hadn't got a quilt. I was in for three weeks that time and don't know what I'd have done if it hadn't been for one of the other prisoners who shared her bedding with me. It was full of lice, they crawled all over me, but I was glad of that quilt all the same. It helped to keep me warm. She was a very poor woman, the one who lent it to me. The poor are very kind.' She paused for a moment, reflecting.

'It was the poor who looked after my friend when she'd been beaten up and turned out of her home. That was years ago, just after the war. The Reds were in control as soon as the Japanese were beaten, and they didn't waste any time. I was living in my friend's home, and we both knew she was on their list. She was a landowner, you see. There was nothing we could do. Only wait. And pray.' She was speaking sombrely now. 'We prayed a lot in those days.'

'Someone said to me, "Why don't you get away while you can? It's her they're after. If you left now you could get away." But I said, "What sort of a person would I be to live in my friend's home when everything's peaceful and then leave her when she's in difficulties?" '

So she had remained on, sharing with her friend the darkness of foreboding as the days passed and whispered reports reached them of this one and that one being subjected to 'the justice of the people'. To escape was impossible, for her friend was a marked woman.

An evening came when the compound was ominously quiet, no servant appeared, and they were alone together in the house. They knew the hour had come. Breathlessly they waited until they heard the sound of shouting coming nearer, then the battering of the outer gate, a crash, and into the courtyard rushed a crowd of men carrying torches and yelling: 'Where is she? Beat her! Beat her to death!'

After that it was like a nightmare. Miss Chang was pushed roughly aside as the men closed round the other woman, dragged her out into the courtyard, tied ropes under her armpits and slung her up under the branches of a tree. Cowering in the background Miss Chang heard the yells and the thuds, saw the surging mob and the up-lifted sticks and rakes, and the figure swinging helplessly, beams of light flashing against the darkness.

When it was all over and the men had gone, Miss Chang crept forward, half-dragging, half-carrying her friend away. She was almost unrecognisable, but she was still alive.

'Did you take her back into the house?' The question was asked in a whisper, though both knew there were no furtive, listening ears in the quiet Mission Home bedroom.

'Oh no, we didn't dare to go back there. I took her to a hovel along the street. She wouldn't let me stay with her. "Go away, go away," she said. "It'll be worse if they find you're helping me." That was when the beggars helped her. They were the only ones who dared to go along. No-one bothered about them. They gave her food and did what they could for her. The poor are very kind,' said Miss Chang again, and continued, 'She was there for days before she was strong enough to get up. She got away from that district eventually. She's in Lanchow now. But I stayed. It was a worrying time, though. In and out of prison. I didn't know what would happen to me. That's when my hair went grey. Those two years were the worst.

'I saw a Roman Catholic priest martyred. I'll never forget it, the smile on his face when he died. Many people saw it – it made a great impression. I was being taken to the police station, and I prayed, "Lord, if I am to die, let me glorify You as he did . . ."'

A young man whom she had helped spiritually came on one occasion and warned her that more trouble was brewing for her. He'd thought of a plan whereby he could get a false road pass for her, so that she could slip away, he told her, and urged her to let him do it. He was surprised when she refused. Why wasn't she willing to accept this way of escape?

'It wouldn't be right for you to deceive your leaders,'

she said. 'Besides, I want to stay here and suffer with my brothers and sisters in Christ. All the other preachers have left, I'm the only one here now.' She felt she could not leave them like sheep without a shepherd. 'If you want to help me, pray for me,' she told him. 'I know I'm not going to die an ordinary death. Pray for me, that when I die I may glorify the Lord, like that Roman Catholic priest.' She continued going round the villages, preaching Jesus and the forgiveness of sins, repentance and restitution. Many people came to her, eager to hear what she had to tell them of the unseen God, and not a few believed. The officials did not like it and she never knew when she would be taken off for further questioning, or sentenced to another term in prison.

This visit to the south was the first time she had been away for years, and it had been like entering another realm, breathing freer, purer air, to gather with a group of like-minded believers for praise and prayer, Bible study and fellowship.

The marvel was that so many others, twenty in all, had managed to obtain the necessary travel permits to come south at the same time, from similar circumstances. They had come in response to invitations from Pastor David Yang, who had sent out a Spiritual Newsletter to church leaders he had known of in the past, in the provinces of Shansi, Hopei and Honan, and they had brought replies giving news of many living churches not heard of for ten years. First they had endured the Japanese invasion, then the Communist regime. The stories of trial and suffering, of imprisonments and restrictions had been lightened by personal records of miracles of healing, of a holy ingenuity in continuing to proclaim the Good News of the Son of God as, divested of status and income, preachers and church leaders had taken to peddling cloth and vegetables, or going with a pack of tools to do odd jobs of carpentering, and visiting scattered believers in the course of earning a livelihood.

'Suffering is never welcomed by man, but suffering can cause a man to know God better,' was a constant theme in the testimonies they gave. 'Suffering has the power to revive backsliders. It is also a good method of purifying the church, since when tribulation comes those who are Christians in name only are winnowed away. Churches merely concerned with external appearances disappear altogether, but those that are true are purified through suffering. One sister was shut up in a cave for several months, and beaten many times. Each time she was beaten until she fainted away with pain. But when revived she said, "The Lord has used these to purge away my inward dross and to remove my iron bars."

'There was a church which, before the civil war, was extraordinarily cold. The pastor there had backslidden to such a degree there was no sin he did not commit, living just like a worldling. But suffering pressed, growing daily more severe, until he could bear it no longer. When he turned and looked to God, he was revived. From that time on he carried his Gospel book-bag, tramping over mountains and across rivers, testifying for our Lord. Although on several occasions he was arrested and cast into prison, when released he preached the Gospel as before. Signs and wonders followed him and believers were added to the Lord. Although they continually met persecution, nevertheless, they increasingly preached the Word.

'We truly want to thank the Lord; suffering is for the profit of God's children. If we want our lives to be beautiful, then we must welcome suffering.'

They did not stay long, those men from the north, with their cultured voices and their homespun clothes that looked strangely out of place in the sophisticated city. They took with them what Bibles and books they could carry, bade farewell to the missionaries they had come to see for the last time, and set out for the long journey homeward, Miss Chang among them.

In her bundles of Bibles and illustrated Christian

posters were a tin of cocoa and some powdered milk. She had accepted them after only a moment's hesitation. It was worth taking the risk of having to explain who gave them to her. 'Now I'll be able to make a cup of cocoa to cheer myself up when things are looking bad,' she remarked with a care-free smile. She was no ascetic idealist, looking for martyrdom, just a robust disciple prepared to take up her cross and follow her Master – all the way.

'Of whom the world was not worthy.'

*   *   *

There was much coming and going on the C.I.M. compound during those early months of 1951, and among those who came to say goodbye were some groups from the Little Flock. Time had been when they had kept strictly apart from western missionary societies, critical of such organisations and their 'unspiritual' methods, but in recent months there had been a noticeable softening of this attitude. The gesture of coming to extend the handshake of fellowship at this time of withdrawal bound up all the breaches of the past. The Little Flock was a movement that had always been free of all foreign influences and independent of foreign financial support, and for that reason it had appeared in the early days of the Communist regime that it would escape the persecution that was coming on other churches. Already, however, it was becoming evident that their adherence to the Gospel and teachings of Christ would bring them into difficulties with the Communist authorities. They were going ahead with their plans in spite of it, and were prepared to talk those plans over with those they had come to see.

The plans were mainly concerned with the evangelisation of China by means of the mass migration of Christians. Groups of Christians with their families were expected to move away together from Shanghai to settle in inland areas, especially where there were no established churches, to earn their living in their own professions or trades, and at the same time to witness for Christ. The congregation of 4-5,000 in Shanghai was a sort of seed-bed from which small but mature church groups would be planted throughout China.

'Only by leaving all and migrating for the Gospel's sake can you prove your unreserved consecration to Christ,' an article in one of their papers had announced, 'and only by mass migration of Christians can the evangelisation of China be completed.' The method had been tried already, not only by the Little Flock, but by other groups as well, notably the Jesus Family in the north, whose effectiveness in establishing agricultural and industrial communities had at first favourably impressed the Communists. The emphasis of the Little Flock was not so much on communal living as communal worship. Its members would continue to earn their own livings in the normal way, but through their united worship and witness aim to win others to Christ. This was the method by which they hoped to evangelise China.

'Do they really know what's going on inland?' some of the missionaries wondered as they listened. 'The opposition to any form of religion, the enforced attendance at classes on Communist doctrines, the exposure of those who cannot accept them, the secret accusation, the arrests, the interrogations . . . the public trials . . . the executions?'

'The pressure from without is great,' said one of them warningly, in a private conversation. The reply was unforgettable.

'The pressure from without is great,' it was agreed. Then came the quiet explanation. 'But the pressure from within is greater.'

Only as the pressure from within continued greater than the pressure from without could any Christian, Chinese or foreigner, hope to stand at all. While moving and inspiring news was coming through from the provinces of the courage and steadfastness of many in the churches, there were disappointing stories, too, of some who were falling away. And the situation in which some of the missionaries now found themselves was so hazardous that the men of Headquarters staff in Shanghai were at once eager and apprehensive as they opened the letters and telegrams that arrived daily.

'So often a telegram received ends with the one word of appeal, "Pray!"' wrote Arnold Lea in a general letter to all who were still in their centres inland. 'We are glad you add that extra word, for it shows the comfort you are receiving from being part of the Mission family, and that you have realised what we here can do to help. Each telegram is brought to the next day's prayer meeting or if serious enough to an emergency prayer meeting and is spread before the Lord. A promise that has been much set before us of late is from Luke 18.8, "I tell you ... He will!"'

As he looked at the map on his wall and drew out his files to study the correspondence before him, one of the difficulties that loomed largest was the handing over of the Mission hospitals. The one in Kaifeng had been disposed of early enough to avoid complications, but those remaining were all producing problems, mainly connected with employees who were being incited to bring accusations against members of staff. It looked as though it might be a long time before all of the missionaries were either exonerated or fined, and allowed to apply for exit visas. The possibility that some might even be imprisoned had to be faced, and the thought of any of them, women particularly, doing time in gaol was alarming.

Then there were the isolated groups who were unexpectedly having exit visas withheld for no evident reason. He thought rather grimly of the four widely separated teams along the rugged Tibetan border in the far west, and remembered the instructions sent to superintendents a few weeks ago to call in immediately those from the most distant places. How little they had foreseen what the reality would be when they had referred to 'an orderly withdrawal!' The plans they had made in such a businesslike way were proving to be entirely beyond their power to put into execution.

Even the evacuation of the children from the school in Kuling wasn't going smoothly, though the letters received from the principal and teachers were cheerful enough, and full of confidence that the Lord would see them through. One incident they recorded provided the Headquarters staff with a burst of exultant laughter. It had to do with the school's cows. There was an urgent need for cash before the money from the renting of the Shanghai property began to flow, and in a remarkable way the school's business manager had been able to sell the cows to tide over the emergency.

'That's an answer to Mrs. Mason's prayer – not a hoof left behind!' they exclaimed, knowing how difficult it had become to dispose of possessions for cash. They were not particularly surprised when such incidents were related in letters, however, for they had all been in the Mission for years, and had seen so many times how practical a thing it is to have faith in God, that although they did their utmost to ensure that financial supplies got through, they were not unduly anxious when they did not. The Lord would provide. What concerned them far more at this time was the effect that the circumstances in which they were living would have on the missionaries who were becoming more and more isolated, and living in an atmosphere of uncertainty and fear.

The Mission was facing something new in its history. Right from the beginning when Hudson Taylor brought his team of inexperienced young men and women from Victorian England to be scattered in twos and threes in inland China, there had been dangers to encounter and privations and hardships to endure. The isolation of living hundreds of miles inland, days and often weeks' journeys from the nearest outpost of western civilisation, the horrors of the Boxer uprising, dangers from rioting and banditry, the perils of the Japanese invasion, had all been part of the Mission's experience.

But this was different. The long drawn out suspense of waiting could no longer be alleviated by useful activity. The life of preaching and teaching, distributing literature, trudging or cycling long journeys to visit outlying areas, all that went to make up the full programme of a missionary's normal routine was ended for most of them. They were more or less confined to their own compounds, many of them, with nothing to do but sort out their possessions, destroy what they could not take with them, write carefully worded letters that would not cause misunderstanding if they fell into the wrong hands, and wait for their visas to be granted.

They all knew that whatever happened to them they could expect no help, no welcome arrival of a fellow-missionary, even to give moral support. In the past, however remotely placed, they had all known that in a desperate situation they could send a request for help and someone would come post-haste, however far the distance to be travelled. That knowledge, the assurance of each member having a rightful claim on the Mission, just as the Mission had a rightful claim on each member, provided an unconscious sense of security that was now being diminished. No fellow-missionary would come, because no fellow-missionary could travel without a permit from the F.A.B., and when that was granted it was only in one direction – towards the border with Hongkong. Permission had been requested for Mrs. Lorang Pettersen to go to Lanchow that she might have her baby delivered in the hospital there. Permission refused. Permission had been requested for Mrs. Don Cunningham to travel for a similar reason. Permission refused.

It was as though everyone was being slowly frozen in, immobilised, separated.

Well, thought Arnold, there are still some things we can do for them. We can make sure their remittances are sent off, that they're not kept short of money – not at this end, anyway. Thank God – plenty of money coming in steadily and surely from the rent of the dear old Mission House. We can go on praying for them – thank God, that channel is always open! And we can go on writing to them – thank God that the Post Office is still operating normally, and letters are getting through.

Letters! They had always been important, his time as Director was largely taken up in dealing with correspondence, but as the weeks passed they took on a quality that was vitalising, like air being supplied to a diver under water. He knew how much it would mean to those beleaguered little groups to get news, and long letters went out to everyone frequently, giving the names of those who had safely arrived in Hongkong, others known to be on the way – and those who were not moving at all.

'The only one of our membership left in Chekiang province is Miss Heath.'

'The Krafts and their fellow-workers are still daily remembered here in prayer . . . A wire from the Iliffs asks for similar support.'

'Our friends in the north-east are held up temporarily over property matters.'

'We still look for news of the three ladies from Sihsien, the only remaining missionaries in Anhwei province.'

'So far no folk have moved from East Szechwan . . .'

How laconic and inadequate were the plain statements of facts, but folk knew enough to realise what lay behind them! 'Our human natures would have things move faster, but we are more and more convinced that God is timing the movements of each one of us.'

He did not write it piously. The confidence had been expressed in a number of the letters that were coming in daily that '*Our times are in His hands*,' and it was a relief to him to know that others felt it, too. It didn't necessarily relieve the sense of concern, but it took the strain out. And it made him love them more. He felt proud of them.

In the late afternoon of 31 March 1951 he sat down rather wearily to write letters. It had been a day of particularly traumatic experiences, starting very early with the careful inspection of room after empty room, followed with the departure for Hongkong, at ten past eight, of two of his closest colleagues, Keeble and Butler, with their wives, for Hongkong.

Fifty minutes later, promptly at nine a.m., had come the formal handing over of the large Mission Home block to the incoming hospital authorities. No more noisy mealtimes in the big dining-room, with the excited chatter drowning even the clatter of plates being piled up at the ends of the tables, no more hymn-singing and praying together in the drawing-room, no more groups standing at the front entrance to bid 'God-speed' to missionaries setting out for the interior! The seventeen of them who still remained were all housed in the flats of the office block, now, with the stenographers taking turns to provide a midday meal for the office staff.

The morning and afternoon had seen the official termination of the employment of Chinese servants on the large compound. 'Each one has now been given a handsome allowance, depending on years of service. In the case of those who have been with us for many years this should be ample to allow them to live comfortably into old age. Chang-San-hsi, who has been a well-known figure for so many years, topped the list with 46 years of service.' It had been hard to say goodbye to some of them.

The day had also been marked by the final issue of the North China Daily News, which had at last obtained permission to close down. He'd miss that, too, the one newspaper in the English language that had appeared so regularly at his breakfast table all the time he'd been in Shanghai. It was a queer feeling to be seeing the winding up of so many affairs, the termination of so much that was familiar.

His eye fell on a calendar, and with a start he remembered something.

'Tomorrow is the anniversary of the day when Bishop and Mrs. Houghton left Shanghai,' he wrote. 'We praise God for news of continued restoration to health and strength which our General Director has been experiencing.' Then he added feelingly:

'What a year this has been since they left us!'

What a year indeed, with the steadily increasing political tension, the publication of the Manifesto, the sudden explosion of anti-western propaganda following the outbreak of the war in Korea, the pressure on the churches, the decision to withdraw ...

What a year for so many of the fellowship, finding themselves more and more isolated, more and more restricted, prevented from doing the one thing they had come to China to do, hemmed in and unable to move, and oppressed by fear of what might happen.

What a year of divine interventions, too, with the well-nigh miraculous provision of money from the very source most unlikely to provide it – the Communist Government – the Eagle flights from Hongkong, the deliverances from death itself for people up-country like Monica Hogben and Mrs. Douglas, taken so suddenly and seriously ill that life had been despaired of. Or of Mrs. Windsor, right here in the Shanghai compound, just a fortnight ago. He wouldn't soon forget being one of the four to carry her limp body on the bed across the compound after midnight, with someone going ahead to open doors, and another walking alongside to hold aloft the bottle of saline solution that had to be kept in position, after that emergency operation in which everything had depended on the skill of the Chinese Christian surgeon who had been on hand to help. Such an experience had brought home to him afresh the normal health hazards that had to be faced in the new setting of a hostile environment. How would they fare if any of the missionaries in the interior, under house arrest, were taken seriously ill with no-one to whom to appeal?

He looked at the large sheet of paper before him on which were typed names of C.I.M. missionaries still in China, neatly listed under their provinces, or under the more hopeful heading of 'In Transit'. It was a relief every time word came through that one more had arrived safely in Hongkong, and he could cross that name off the list. There had been six hundred and thirty-seven on 1 January 1951. Now, three months later, there were still nearly four hundred, and they were moving out more slowly.

'I shan't go until they've all got their exit visas,' he said to himself. 'I couldn't get out and leave them.' He wondered how long it would be.

It was just about the same time that Harry Gould and his wife Elizabeth decided to resign from the Mission. A sturdy, matter-of-fact Australian couple, they'd been on the staff at Shanghai ever since the Communist take-over, and with the departure of Fred Keeble to Hongkong, Harry was in charge of the accounts. All the same, they agreed together that the time had come to get out.

'Oh, no, we're not leaving China,' Harry told Arnold. 'I'm going to get an accountant's job with Butterfield and Swire.' The well-known shipping firm had its offices in Shanghai, and Harry's duties had frequently taken him there. 'It's like this,' he went on to explain. 'We can do more for the Mission outside than inside now. We're going to stay around as long as any of the Mission are in China. We can see about the rent from the premises, and sending off the remittances and all that sort of thing just as easily outside as inside—better, in fact. The Commies won't take any notice of a mere Aussie employee in a secular business.' They believed the Lord was guiding them to do it, though they didn't say much about that aspect of the case. 'It's you imperialistic missionaries who are the suspects, you know!' They both made light of the whole affair, refusing to see anything noble about what they planned to do.

'What I want now is a game of tennis,' said Elizabeth, picking up her racquet. 'Who'll come along and make up a four?'

CHAPTER SEVEN

The Hindquarters

IT IS ONE thing for the captain to remain on the bridge when the ship is wrecked, directing operations until everyone else is safely in the life-boats before leaving himself. It is another thing for the captain to remain doggedly on the bridge when the ship was broken up, and he has no more control over anything. As spring gave way to summer Arnold Lea, still in Shanghai, had to face the fact that he was in rather that sort of position. By mid-July, having waved off the last two members of the H.Q. staff, he returned alone to the small top-storey flat the hospital committee were allowing him to use. All the eastern provinces now were clear of C.I.M. missionaries, except for the Guinnesses in Nanking, who were comfortably housed though restricted, and the three women in Anhwei who were having a really bad time of it. As far as he could make out, after having had their exit visas taken from them when they were at the point of leaving, they were camping out on the verandah and in the corridors of the mission home, all the rooms having been sealed up. They didn't know when they would get away now.

How thankful he was when at last they received permission to leave and he was able to help them on their way as they passed through Shanghai, en route for Hongkong!

Apart from that, the majority of those still left in China were a thousand miles away, and would not come to Shanghai at all. In the south-west some of the men were under house arrest, a doctor was facing serious charges, in

Szechwan Don Cunningham was in prison, and others living under the threat of it. On the Tibetan border Dr. Rupert Clarke was alone, having been held back at the last moment while the rest of his team were sent on their way. He'd been in gaol for some days. The other groups in the same province, Tsinghai, were given no permission to apply for exit visas.

In Lanchow Leonard Street was pleading in vain with the authorities to grant exit visas to his missionaries, especially the Saunders who'd been waiting for months, and Marie Huttenlock, the young American left alone in the leprosarium across the river. No reason had been given why their exit visas were withheld when others were allowed to leave, and they were left wondering what the authorities would bring up against them. It was particularly hard on Marie, battling with her fears alone. He was fearful that he would have to go before them, dreaded the thought of passing by bus on his way to Hongkong through the little town where Nina Pettersen, nearly nine months pregnant, was living with her husband and little girl in one small room. To go on and leave them there . . .!

Yet if the authorities gave you your exit visa and you didn't leave, you knew you'd forfeited it, and who knew when they'd give you another? The sooner you could get out the better for your Chinese friends who were being harassed continually because you were still around.

The grip of the Government on the Church was tightening, and in a very subtle way, for the 'Three-Self' formula of the missionary movement of a quarter of a century before was adopted – with a new emphasis.

Self-governing meant throwing off the Imperialists' control.

Self-supporting meant throwing off the Imperialists' money.

Self-propagating meant throwing out the Imperialists' poisonous doctrine. If emissaries from the imperialist nations in the form of missionaries were still around, it was evident you hadn't come into line with the policy of the 'Oppose-America, Aid-Korea, Three Self Reform Movement of the Church of Christ in China'.

Trying to wind twelve carbon sheets into his typewriter, with the gas stove as filing cabinet and nowhere to hang his wet clothes except on a bamboo pole stuck out of the window, Arnold realised that his position was ludicrous! Whatever was happening to any of his fellow missionaries, he couldn't move a finger to help them. All he could do was write letters. The only effect his presence in Shanghai was having was to make things a bit more difficult for the Chinese who knew him.

Meanwhile, he was receiving letters almost daily, urging him to come to Hongkong as soon as possible. 'You're really needed here,' he was told. 'You're the one who should be around to represent the missionaries when top-level decisions have to be made by the Directors. You ought to be meeting up with them as they come out of China. We need you here. All these plans for launching out into new work in new countries . . . You should be on hand, to find out what the missionaries themselves are feeling about it.'

Even more urgent, perhaps, was the matter of relationships with the governments of the countries of South-East Asia into which C.I.M. missionaries were now being deployed. The old days of colonial rule were over, and new nations were being born with new laws, new policies, and often very suspicious views of westerners. They wouldn't be too eager for another missionary society to enter without being very clear as to what it intended to do.

Mission comity, too. In most places in China C.I.M. had been first on the field, the pioneering mission with which new societies had sought to co-operate. Now the situation was reversed, and C.I.M. would be the new-comer. In many places the pioneering stage was already past, and C.I.M. missionaries were being invited to fit into an established work. It was going to be a perplexing job, needing delicate handling, to get everyone fitted into the right niche.

'You know our folk better than anyone else. You're the one they look to now that J.R.S. has retired. You were appointed China Director in his place. You ought to be here.'

Everything pointed to it now. He realised that. When, in July, he was told that he could apply for his exit visa he knew he must do so.

'Take it while you can, Arnold!' The Goulds urged. 'You'll be lucky to get away, when so many of the head men in various organisations and firms are having real difficulties, being held up for months. You can't do anything more for our folk. We're seeing to the money side of things, and that's all anyone can do. You go while the going's good! You're needed in Hongkong.'

He applied for his visa, but the thought of leaving while others were still held weighed heavily with him.

One day, kneeling in prayer, going one by one over the names of the eighty and more C.I.M. missionaries who still remained in China, he lifted his head and his eyes alighted on the calendar on the wall. 'I will never leave them nor forsake them' he read, and it was as though Someone had spoken direct to him, there in the empty room. Minutes later he realised that he had mis-read it, putting 'them' where it was really 'thee', but the message had got through.

'I don't know how many times during this week the text on my wall, which last time I told you I had learned to read wrongly, has been a consolation to me,' he wrote the day before he left Shanghai for the border. 'It is with every mixed feelings that I contemplate going, for I do not relish the thought of, as it were, leaving you behind. One feels a bit cheap, as if running away . . . But He has said, 'I will not fail them, nor forsake them'. I may be appearing to forsake, but the One who really counts is with you each one . . .'

It was a comfort to him as he packed his bags and prepared to leave.

When eventually he walked past the last barbed wire barrier over the iron bridge spanning the ditch-like stream that marked the boundary between China and the Crown Colony of Hongkong, saw the Union Jack fluttering on a high pole, the food trolleys displaying Coca Cola and Cadbury's Milk Chocolate, heard the animated chatter of people on the platform waiting for the train to take them to Kowloon, it was like entering another world from the one he had just left, with its 'Love China – Hate America' campaign, its loud-speakers incessantly propagating Communist doctrines, its silent queues and its unsmiling officials. The welcome he received from the Mission group was heart-warming, and he sensed the eagerness with which they snatched at every bit of news that came out of China, setting off for the border every time there was the possibility of someone else arriving.

There was an air of optimism about the group in Hongkong. 'God's timing has been perfect!' they said again and again. Freehaven had been provided just when numbers coming out were large, then as people came more slowly and wearied with the strain, a house on one of the islands had been acquired that was ideal for providing folk with a short holiday before sending them on their way. They had seen a definite pattern in it all – first the eastern provinces being cleared, then an influx from the southwest and so on, never too many arriving at once, always passages out obtained in time for the next lot to be accommodated. 'Our times *are* in His hands!'

And the stories they had heard! The way that dog from a local inn came and lay every day for a fortnight before the door of the room where Nina Pettersen was confined after the birth of her second baby. That dog didn't like Communist cadres. Every time one approached the hair on its back began to bristle, and its throat began to snarl. The cadres had been in the habit of walking in and out of the room as they pleased, but they didn't like the look of that dog and kept out. The Pettersens obtained their exit visas soon after that, arriving safely in Hongkong about three weeks after Leonard Street.

He had been peremptorily informed he must leave Lanchow on 1 August, the next day. It was a special day, commemorating a Communist anniversary, and the plans for it included the military taking over the hospital to which the leprosarium was attached. To leave Marie alone there in those circumstances! Leonard's prayers to God and pleas to man prevailed. All right, she could go too. The following morning he boarded the bus with her, en route for the border. The loneliness, the uncertainty, the horror of seeing lines of men, chained together, pass along the road outside the hospital, on their way to the execution ground, were over for her at last.

Or take the Hogarths in Kweichow. They were given exactly twenty days to get out of the country, and they knew that all the boats down the Yangtze would be full, and they would probably have to wait weeks before obtaining a booking. But they reached Chungking at Chinese New Year, and there were a few last minute cancellations of Chinese not wanting to travel on that day, with the consequence that the Hogarths got away in time to arrive at the border on the twentieth day after their passes had been issued.

And the people you'd have thought were too frail to travel, like old Miss Petersen who hadn't been out of her room for months, or Annie Skau whose haemoglobin count was so low you wondered she could survive. Yet they had arrived safely, as had Dorothy Woodward with her leg in plaster. God was bringing them out of China, one by one, and with His hand on them nothing could stop them.

It was like being on the right side of the tapestry to be in Hongkong, where the pattern of things was so clearly seen, and where there was such a bright hope for the future. There was much talk about the new avenues of service opening up all over South-East Asia, of some who were already evangelising right here in Hongkong, in Borneo, in the Philippines. God still had a plan for the Mission, a work for it to do. Onward into Malaya, Thailand, Japan . . .!

When it came to thinking about new countries, Arnold found his mind did not react favourably. He could not forget the land he had left behind, the men and women there who knew that suffering for Christ rather than service for Him was now their appointed lot, his own fellow-missionaries waiting in the strain of uncertainty and isolation. He looked at the list he kept with him of those still left behind, and saw that by the end of September there were still seventy-five of them. 'Let me assure you that much prayer is being made for you by name continually and also for those we so dearly love in the Lord,' he wrote, ending with the words, 'Still with you much in thought, spirit and understanding.'

He was out of China now, he realised, but it would be a long, long time before China was out of him.

* * *

The Mission home in Chungking had always been the scene of much coming and going, with the river steamers bringing people up from the coast, through the breath-taking beauty of the Yangtze gorges, to scatter from Chungking to their various centres westward and northward and southward, in Szechwan province itself and also to Yunnan and Kweichow. A big, sprawling old house on the thickly populated hillside, it was an exhausting business climbing slowly up the winding cobbled street to reach it, and Chris Ellison had to do plenty of it that autumn of 1951. He was the missionary in charge now that Toliver had left, and what with visits to the F.A.B. to help people get their exit visas, visits to the police station to answer innumerable quesions and fill in innumerable forms, visits to the river side to help folk with their baggage as they boarded the steamers that would take them down-river (all going in the same direction now!) he felt he knew every open drain to be stepped over, and every rat-ridden pot-hole to be avoided. The thick humidity didn't make exercise any easier, nor the smells any less penetrating, either.

There had been more of it to do now that Lucy, the young Communist in charge of their affairs at the F.A.B., had peremptorily instructed Toliver to come and get his exit visa by four-thirty in two days' time, or she'd show him something. The punctiliously polite but nonchalant American had irritated her beyond measure by explaining, every time she asked him why he didn't apply for his own exit visa, that he didn't want to go yet. She wanted to see the back of him, and as the afternoon wore on her indignation mounted until when he eventually arrived her eyes were blazing and her chest heaving. The Death Squad, the same four soldiers who had arrived a few days before to take off one of the 49ers to gaol for a misdemeanour against the People, was lined up against the wall. It looked dramatic.

'Why didn't you come earlier?' she stormed. As though he didn't know how long it took to get through the formalities of issuing an exit visa!

'Well you see,' Toliver replied, 'the limit set was Thursday, four-thirty p.m., and it is now ten minutes past four. Here I am.' If Lucy could have found a reason for handing him over to the Death Squad, it was obvious she would have done so, but she knew there was no reason. The officials in charge of foreigners' affairs in the bigger cities were well-trained and experienced, generally carrying out their duties strictly according to the letter of the law, and Lucy was no exception. She might be unnecessarily stern (though on occasion she was quite gracious) but she was just. Breathing heavily she pushed a form across to him and told him to fill it in. As always, he obeyed, and when she had glanced through it she scribbled a few characters on a slip of paper, stamped it with red, and almost threw it at him.

'This pass allows the holder to leave the People's Republic of China and return to his own country,' it read. 'It does not permit him ever to return to China again.'

He'd set up a record of sorts, he laughed afterwards, for surely that was the shortest waiting time for any exit permit ever issued – two minutes! For personal reasons he was glad enough to go, for his wife and two small children, and the baby he had not yet seen, were waiting for him. All the same, he hadn't wanted to leave – not while there were still so many to be helped as they passed through Chungking on their way to freedom. It was over to Ellison now. He could do no more.

'The hindquarters!' That was how Chris Ellison described himself. With Arnold Lea in Hongkong, there was no longer a Headquarters in China, but while there was someone to see to business affairs in Chungking, the centre through which at least half of those still remaining would have to pass, he ought to have some sort of a designation. Hindquarters seemed appropriate.

Chris Ellison didn't feel he was really cut out for the job, since preaching and teaching rather than administration was his line. For that reason he had accepted the position somewhat reluctantly, but now that he was in it he intended to stick it out. Years before, when it had become obvious that the Communists would gain control of the country, he had had a pang of fear so real and so deep that it had alarmed him. He hadn't tried to disguise his feeling, or to rationalise it. That wasn't the way to deal with it, as he very well knew. So he had got down on his knees, and prayed to his God, and then steadied his mind by dwelling on some of the promises he had so often quoted in his sermons. After that the fear had gone, and never returned, not even during the horrifying days of this 'Year of the Purge', when lists of names were pasted up on the city walls daily of those arrested, and a red mark alongside those who were executed. It was whispered with bated breath that there had been as many as a thousand arrests in one day. Always there were bodies lying on the banks of the Yangtze until darkness fell, when relatives stole silently along to take them off and bury them.

He knew the same sort of thing was going on all over China, and that the missionaries living in the smaller places were much closer to it all, and living under far greater strain than he and Catherine. He thought of the four men in Kweiyang, still waiting in vain for their exit visas, though their wives had got away months before. He thought of Chengtu, where the large concentration of missionaries of various societies was rapidly being reduced, but where the Vindens and Gordon Harman were facing accusations and had no permission to apply for exit visas. The Iliffs, in their centre, were evidently having an even more difficult time, called up night after night for interrogation, while as for those on the Tibetan border in Tsinghai province, seven of them and two small children, they seemed stuck without the hope of a move, and Dr. Rupert Clarke, who was alone, hadn't been heard of for weeks.

Worse still, in a way, was the thought of the women who were having to face things alone, like Lilian Fletcher and Stella Bills with forty soldiers billeted on their compound, or Irene Cunningham with her three small children, and her husband Don in prison. The two younger women missionaries who were with her had refused to apply for their exit visas when told they could do so, unwilling to leave her, but what if the authorities insisted?

Chris and Catherine Ellison agreed they must remain on in Chungking, even after they'd been moved into a smaller building and could no longer have the transients to stay. They were the only members of the Mission left now in this central place of contact. Also, there was a great pile of baggage still to be disposed of, trunks and boxes that had been left behind to be sent on when convenient. It was part of the business manager's job to send them down river as opportunity arose. The pile was diminishing slowly, each group of missionaries travelling out taking responsibility for some to go along with their own belongings. So when he learned that Lilian Fletcher and her companion had at last obtained their exit visas and had already arrived at the inn near the quay, waiting to embark on a vessel going down river, he got in touch with them. Could they take along a few trunks belonging to other missionaries? They had been officially searched by the Communist authorities and were duly stamped, so would not need to be opened again. With the official seal on them there would be no more formalities to go through. It was just a matter of seeing they were duly deposited in Hongkong.

Lilian Fletcher agreed to be responsible for them. It was the sort of thing fellow-missionaries did for each other, and now that Stella and she were on their way out she was glad to help someone else by bringing out some of their belongings for them. She checked the items, saw the official sign on each, and thought no more about them.

It was over two years since she had been in Chungking, where she had accompanied Stella so that the latter could meet her fiance, one of the newly arrived 49ers, and from there the two of them had gone on to the town of Kiangtsing, to work with the little group of Christians there. To everyone's surprise, the town had been captured by the Communists twelve days after their arrival, and they had been cut off for weeks without receiving any mail. They were almost at the end of their resources when a Post Office official, guessing their need, insisted on giving them half of the weekly salary he had just received. It was sufficient to tide them over until communications were opened up again. God could provide the right help at the right time! After that things went fairly smoothly for a while, but with the outbreak of the war in Korea and the publishing of the Manifesto, liberty was gradually withdrawn. The pastor of the church was imprisoned, the anti-American feeling in the town was whipped up, and they knew that they themselves were a liability to the Christians. It was with relief that they heard many missionaries were getting away, and that soon they would be allowed to go, too.

Then they were called to Party Headquarters and questioned. 'Who are the aggressors in the Korean war?' was the main interrogation, and when neither of them agreed that America was the culprit the atmosphere became increasingly hostile. Stoutly they refused to acquiesce to all the Communist ideology that was propounded, either, and when the long interview ended they were told they would not be receiving the exit visas they had been promised. They must wait till a later date.

From that time on things took a definite turn for the worse. Unable any longer to continue preaching and teaching, they had opened a simple clinic in which they treated abscesses and boils, cuts and burns. They had been careful to avoid giving away any medicine, but all the same the local doctors accused 'the imperialists' of taking away their trade, so they had to close down. They could no longer do anything to help anybody.

The police started pestering them, arriving at midnight to bang on the gates and demand an entrance. They searched the rooms time and again, going through their books and papers, searching for some evidence on which the foreigners could be arrested. But they found none.

Then the compound was taken over by the military. With forty soldiers billeted on their property, the two women found themselves allocated one small room. It had previously been the pantry. In the steamy heat of summer it was not easy to sit in it, day after day, with nothing to do but wait, fighting the fears that assailed them as they wondered what would happen to them. No longer free to attend Sunday services, they held one of their own in their tiny room, singing hymns together while the soldiers next door jeeringly tried to drown their voices by bawling patriotic songs.

Stella thought of her fiancé, now in Hongkong, and wondered if she would ever see him again.

'I have been encouraged lately in my morning reading to realise afresh that God's help and blessing are dependent, not on any outstanding ability or human power, but on simple reliance on Himself and His Word,' wrote Lilian about that time, in a letter home. '*The children of Israel prevailed because they relied on the Lord God of their fathers.*' 2 Chron. 13.8. And in the back of her Bible she wrote a quotation she came across:

'Leave it all quietly with God, my soul.
My rescue comes from Him alone.
Rock, Rescue, Refuge, He is all to me,
Never shall I be overthrown.'

They needed that inward confidence. On the occasions when they ventured out into the street to go to the Post Office they were likely to be followed by crowds of children yelling 'Kill the foreigners! Kill the foreigners!' And on the walls of the Post Office photos were displayed of men kneeling in line on the beach of the Yangtze, hands tied behind their backs, waiting to be shot . . .

The only visitor they had now was a courageous Christian woman who had been reduced to hawking goods for a living, and this provided her with the only reason she dared to give for going to see them.

'The foreigners may be needing soap, or something I can sell them,' she said to the guards at the gate. With the tray of goods around her neck she was allowed to pass in, and once alone with the two missionaries she would quietly give them all the news.

'The peasants who have had their landlords' land given to them aren't so happy now – they find they have to hand most of what they produce over to the Communists.

'They say twenty people a day are being shot . . . Mr. Li who lived in our street was shot last night. So was Mr. Wang who ran the corner shop . . . The pastor, in prison, is very ill . . .'

They applied time and time again for an exit visa, waiting for hours outside the F.A.B. office until, having obtained an entrance, they were refused. At last, however, late in September, they had been given permission to start the necessary procedure by advertising their proposed departure in the paper. They obtained guarantors, were eventually handed their exit visas, and on 14 October had said goodbye to the little group of Christian women who had come to the riverside to see them off. 'God be with you till we meet again,' they had sung quietly together, tears streaming down their faces. 'The Communists can take away our goods, but they can't take the Lord Jesus out of our hearts.'

So they parted. It was a farewell the two missionaries would never forget.

They had a thousand-mile journey ahead of them. First there was the river trip to Chungking where they must get a booking on a Yangtze steamer to Hankow, then by train to Canton and on to the border, beyond which lay Hongkong – and freedom.

All went well. They added seventeen pieces of baggage to their own three pieces in Chungking, reached the border without incident, and were perparing to follow the coolies taking the luggage up to the final barrier when they realised something was wrong. The baggage was all being carried back, and they were sternly informed that they could not cross over the border that day. Something had come to light which must be investigated, and they would not be permitted to proceed until the matter was cleared up.

'But what is it?' asked Lilian. 'Our papers are in order, and all the baggage we have with us has been examined and sealed. What is wrong?'

'Look at this!' She was shown a small notebook. 'This was found in one of the trunks you brought from Chungking.'

'But there's nothing in it,' she said, turning over the empty pages.

'Look at the back!' She turned to the back, and inside

the last page she saw a single sentence, written in Chinese characters, followed by six Chinese names. She read it with a gasp of dismay. It was sufficient to brand the owner as a spy.

'The people of China oppose the Communist Revolution!'

It has been said that crises do not make the man – they merely reveal him. This crisis, coming so unexpectedly when freedom was within sight, gave Lilian Fletcher no time for reflection. Standing there in the great bare Customs house, with its anti-American posters all round the wall, its armed guards and its grim-faced officials, the incriminating notebook in her hand, she caught a sight of her young companion's face and made up her mind. Turning to the official she said:

'All this has nothing to do with her. Her papers are in order, and her fiancé is waiting for her on the other side of that bridge. Please let her go. I'm the one who took responsibility for this baggage, not she. I'm the only one who should remain behind.'

There was no time for remonstrances. Scarcely realising what was happening Stella moved on to the border while Lilian, a quick prayer in her heart, turned back into China.

* * *

The prayer meeting held in Freehaven that evening was intense and prolonged. The thought of their fellow-missionary on the other side of the border, alone in a city where she was a stranger, with that incriminating sentence found in the luggage for which she was responsible burdened the minds of all. How was it that notebook had been overlooked in Chungking? And why, with the official seal on it, had the trunk been re-opened? There had been a cat and mouse element in affairs before, with missionaries receiving exit visas only to have them cancelled at the last minute, but this was the first time one of them had been turned back at the border. What new move was this? Had the notebook been deliberately planted?

Whatever the explanation, one thing was certain. Lilian Fletcher was held in China, facing a possible charge of spying, and there was nothing anyone could do to come to her aid. They would not even know what was happening to her. Only God could help her now.

CHAPTER EIGHT

Help Those Women!

LILIAN SAT on the hard bed in the upstairs room where she had spent the night, and drew her New Testament from her handbag. Outside, the calls of food vendors and shouts of coolies betokened the dawning of another day, and the habit of years asserted itself, even in the strange circumstances in which she found herself. She must start the day with God. If ever she had been in conscious need of Him, it was now.

She had passed through the experiences of the past few hours almost without realising what was happening. One little incident stood out after Stella had left and she was still waiting in the Customs shed. An agent of the China Travel Service, who a short time before had changed their money into Hongkong dollars, came to her and said quietly:

'I wish I could help you, but I can't. You haven't even got your suitcase with you now, have you? There's one thing I can do. I've got a new face cloth at home that I haven't used. I'll go and get it for you.' The face cloth had been useful and she was thankful for it, but it was the simple act of human kindness that had helped to alleviate the growing sense of her helplessness in the midst of official hostility. But now the numbness that follows shock was passing, and fears of what the future held threatened to agitate her.

'I must keep calm,' she thought and started turning over the pages of the New Testament, looking for the verses that spoke of peace.

'We have peace with God . . .'

'The peace of God which passeth all understanding shall keep your hearts and minds through Christ Jesus.'

'My peace I give unto you . . .'

She read them slowly, trying to concentrate on them, but then her eye fell on another verse that gripped her immediately.

'The God of peace shall be with you.' This was different. It did not so much refer to a quality as to a Person. The God of peace Himself – with her. Wherever she was taken, whatever accusations were levelled against her, however impossible she found it to understand this southern Chinese dialect of Cantonese, through it all the God of peace would go with her. God the Creator – on her side! God who brought order out of chaos – with her. 'If the God of peace is with me, then everything will be under His control,' she thought. 'I'll just leave it all to Him, and not try to make plans.' The peace for which she had prayed submerged her. She tidied herself, ate the bowlful of rice brought to her, and waited.

In the middle of the morning she was taken to the railway with an armed guard. She could not remain here, she was told. She was being sent to Canton, for questioning.

How would she manage, she wondered, with everyone talking Cantonese around her, which she did not understand. Alone with her silent guard she sat in the train that was taking her away from freedom, back into China. But she refused to worry. The God of peace was with her, and He would bring peace.

At the Police Station in Canton, to her relief, there was a Mandarin-speaking official, and his attitude towards her, right from the start, was unobtrusively friendly. He came from North China, he told her, and his mother was a Christian. He was on hand to help in explaining the questions put to her, and when the time came for her to be put into custody he went with her in the Black Maria to the hotel for political prisoners.

'You will be kept here until the matter of the notebook is cleared up,' he told her. He did not know how long that would be, or what would be the outcome. Well, her overnight case had been given to her, she had her New Testament, and she settled down to wait. 'Lord,' she said, 'I'm willing to trust You all the way, even if it means going right back to Kiangtsing . . .' But she tried not to dwell on that possibility.

Two days later an official arrived in her room. She could leave, she was told coldly. No explanations were given, but the matter of the notebook had been cleared up. She was free, she could go, she was no longer in custody. How was she to get back to the border? That was her affair! 'Lord,' she murmured silently, 'it's *Your* affair!'

Looking across the road she saw a China Travel Agency office, and her heart leapt. They would be able to help her there. They were accustomed to dealing with westerners, and C.I.M. missionaries had often been among their clients. She crossed the road and went into the office to see about getting a railway ticket to the border.

The man at the desk looked at her, scrutinised her papers, then shook his head.

'Your exit visa has expired,' he said. 'You can't get out of China now – in fact, you won't even be allowed to board the train in Canton to go to the border.'

'. . . But the God of peace was with me!' exclaimed Lilian a couple of days later, relating her experiences to the excited crowd gathered around her in Freehaven. 'A member of the Travel Agency staff went with me to the appropriate Communist office, and was able to obtain a temporary exit pass for me. He also took me to an inn near the Canton station so that I could spend the night there and catch an early morning train to the border. This time I was able to cross the bridge without incident and come on by train to Hongkong – and freedom!' Then, with face aglow, she concluded:

'The God of peace has been with me all the way!'

About the same time, in the thickly populated city of Changsha in central China, William and Beatrice Ebeling were facing the hardest ordeal of their lives. His exit visa was refused, but she had just been told she must leave the country at once, taking their two little girls with her. She was expecting their third child in about two months' time, and the prospect of her travelling alone, facing the crowds who always came swarming round to see white children, uncertain at what stage she might be taken off by officials for questioning, was alarming in the extreme. But there was no way out. William managed to make an arrangement with the China Travel Agency to provide an escort, and when he returned from seeing them off, not knowing what the future held for him, he realised he had already touched rock-bottom. Interrogations, arrest, imprisonment, nothing would ever be quite so bad as seeing his peculiarly defenceless little family swallowed up in the sea of Chinese humanity, where patriotism could be exhibited convincingly by fierce shouts of 'Hate the Americans! Kill the foreigners!'

For the four men under house arrest in Kweiyang in the south-west it was not quite so bad, for their wives were already safely in Hongkong. But it was a strain, not knowing what they would have to endure before they were reunited. *If* they were ever reunited . . .

For David Day, in Chungking, the prospect of being reunited was much more slender. He had already been in prison for weeks, having made the mistake of taking a firm hand with a gang of troublesome youngsters who were making things hard for the 49ers in their bungalows on the hills, his own young bride among them. All the missionaries took warning from that incident. Whatever physical attacks were made on you or yours, you'd better put up with them, or you might land yourself in jail.

It was easier said than done, however, when you saw your senior missionary, old enough to be your father, viciously smacked again and again in the face by an angry-

eyed young pastor who had been successfully indoctrin-
ated, and was showing his indignation against 'the
imperialists'. Gordon Harman did not stop to consider
the wisdom or otherwise of intervening. He went straight
at the assailant and dragged him off, helped in the ensuing
scuffle by one or two sympathetic by-standers.

'Very good of you, Gordon,' said Gilbert Vinden afterwards. 'But you shouldn't have done it. If anything like
that happens again, don't move a finger yourself. Call for
help. Let the Chinese deal with it. We've got to learn to
turn the other cheek – quite literally.' He spoke feelingly.
The practical outworking of the ethics of the Sermon on
the Mount was something he was learning in these days.
Strange how long one can go on in the Christian ministry
without realising how far short one falls of the ideal!
That young pastor repeatedly used the word 'Imperialist!'
when raging at him—a word that stood for pride and
arrogance in the Communist's estimation.

'Proud and arrogant—fond of my own way, not willing
to defer to others?' Vinden asked himself, and was
reminded of the words, 'Take my yoke upon you and learn
of Me; for I am meek and lowly in heart.' This experience
of being deprived of authority, having to ask permission
to do this and that, being publicly insulted, was hard, but
perhaps it was necessary? 'The Lord has been sending us
to school, and the subject of this class is meekness,' he said
later. To accept the humiliations and strains in that light
helped to take the sting out of them.

Similar thoughts were occurring to Arthur Mathews
in the small town of Hwangyuan in Tsinghai, on the wind-
swept Tibetan border. The authorities in that obscure
place took a special pleasure in mortifying the foreigner in
their midst. When he went to apply for his exit visa he was
kept waiting for hours outside the office before being
insolently informed that it would not be issued yet. Now
another indignity was being heaped on him. The money
that was being sent to him through the bank from Shanghai

was frozen. He could not draw it out without police permission. He was down to fifteen cents when he went along to ask meekly for the money that was his by right. Instead of the money he was told to go and write out a full report – in Chinese character.

If he had had only himself to consider he would probably have argued about it and risked the consequences, but with a wife and two-year-old daughter dependent on him he had no option. It was one of the many occasions when what he had written in a letter home earlier was put to the test.

'These trials of faith are to give us patience, for patience can only be worked as faith goes into the Pressure Chamber. To pull out because the pressure is laid on, and to start fretting would be to lose all the good He has in it for us.'

When he had laboriously written out the report and taken it back to the police station an underling took it from him, stuffed it into his pocket and said casually:

'All right, go home. This is our affair.'

'Some money?' But there would be no money released until the report had been studied, he was told. 'Go home.'

It was one of Arthur's worst moments. He turned away, and walked slowly back to the cold room in which they were living, where they lit a fire morning and evening to cook food and get what warmth they could for a short time. Their food supply had almost run out, their fuel also. And it would probably take the police weeks to study that report. Oh, God! If You don't step in now! ...

*   *   *

Hundreds of miles across the mountains, down in Chungking, Chris Ellison was clearing up as best he could in preparation for departure for the border. He and Catherine had applied for their exit visas at last, and knew that when they were granted they could delay no longer. There was nothing they could do now to help the others in the south-west who were still waiting to get away. He wrote to them all, gave them instructions about drawing their remittances from the bank, sent them all a blank cheque which they could fill in for whatever sum they might require in an emergency, told them what inn to go to when they arrived in Chungking, and where to book their passages down-river. Having gone carefully through the list of those for whom he had responsibility he sat back and looked at his accounts. There was still about forty-five U.S. dollars left over, and he wondered how he should use it.

Suddenly he remembered the Mathews up in the north-west. They'd been having a tough time of it for months, and he'd heard that now they were having difficulty draw-ing the money sent to them from Shanghai. The bank was frozen.

Well, if the bank has frozen up on them, he thought the Post Office hasn't. Letters are still getting through, so why not telegrams? It was worth trying, anyway.

He went along to the Post Office, handed over the money, and said easily:

'Will you telegraph this to Mr Mathews in Hwang-yuan, Tsinghai, please?' The money was accepted with-out question, the necessary form filled in, and Ellison walked out. Some weeks later, having arrived safely in Hongkong, he learned that the money had been waiting for Mathews on the very day he returned dejectedly from the police station.

* * *

Irene Cunningham looked round the dingy little room where the two young women missionaries had slept, next to the one that she occupied with the three children, and noted its emptiness. They had really gone now. For weeks it had been hanging over them, the consciousness that they might have to go and leave her. The first time the authori-ties had suggested it they had said no, they wouldn't go unless Mrs. Cunningham could go too. But when, later on, they had again been told to apply for their exit visas, they had all agreed it would be better for them to do so. The same sort of thing was happening in other places. It was very rare for a complete group to obtain their exit visas at once. In the case of the 49ers, for instance, it had been decided that the girls should get out first, and theirs had been the first applications made for exit visas, the men putting in for theirs several weeks later. But it was the men who got their visas first, and they had the mortification of packing up and leaving the girls behind. The girls, however, had got away soon afterwards. Once there was a move of any sort, it seemed to be a good sign. So the two young women missionaries had left in their mountain chairs, looking back at her ruefully over their shoulders as they were carried along the dusty street towards the Police Station where Don was imprisoned. They had to fill in more papers there before proceeding. Would they have got a glimpse of him, she wondered? Would he have seen or heard them, and know they were leaving?

It was six months since he'd been arrested and marched off to jail, and she had not seen him since. She had merely been told by the police to take him food twice a day. The three of them had taken turns to do that, walking through the town with the food she'd cooked, everyone seeing them and knowing where they were going. It had meant being shouted after occasionally, by youngsters who were learning patriotic songs and imbibing Communist 'anti-imperialist' doctrines. For the most part the people in the town were silently sympathetic, for who knew how soon any of them would be in the same position?

Well, now that the two girls had gone, she'd have to take the food herself every time, thought Irene. She'd have her hands full, doing all the cooking and cleaning and marketing, looking after the children and remembering to bake a cake each Saturday, so Don would know what day of the week it was. She could expect no help from anyone, for although occasionally one of the Christians would steal in to talk to her, they had to do it secretly, and she knew that in some cases their conditions were even worse than her own. The pastor's wife, for instance, whose husband had been imprisoned some time before Don was taken off, and had been sent home six months later so ill that he died before he even got there.

It had all come so suddenly in the end, the girls leaving. They'd been given only three days to get out, and somehow they had all felt it was impossible that she and the children would be left behind. Something would happen, Don would be released, or she'd get her exit visa, or the girls would be held up after all. But everything had gone as arranged, they were on their way to Chungking, and she was alone with the children, with no more expectation of relief for Don or herself than when he was taken off.

'The situation's so desperate it's almost funny,' she had said once or twice, for her sense of humour frequently got the better of her and carried her soaring over difficulties like a thoroughbred taking fences. Even she could not see anything to chuckle over now, however, so there was really no explaining the joy that bubbled up within her from time to time, a joy too exquisite and deep for laughter. There was no explaining her lack of fear, either, for there was plenty to make her afraid, especially after she was left alone and youths started pelting her little mud house with stones, and storming inside to curse and even spit at her. Things got to such a pass sometimes that she felt she would have to go to the police station and ask for protection. Even then it wasn't fear, just commonsense that urged her to do it, but then a verse of Scripture came to her mind and held her back.

'*Woe unto them that go down to Egypt for help.*' All right. She'd do nothing, only trust.

The way of deliverance from that particular trial came in an unlooked-for manner. She was taken ill, running a high temperature and vomiting. Too exhausted to move, she had to tell the children how to make the food, giving them instructions weakly from her bed. The stone-throwing stopped abruptly, and she learned later that the youngsters responsible had been taken to task about it. 'We serve the Living God,' she said, 'no matter what the Lord asks me to do now, I know He will supply the grace, and whatever it is I need.'

One day she was too exhausted to pray. 'Lord,' she murmured, 'put it in someone's mind at home to pray for us now. I can't . . .' She still managed to keep a brief record of events, and made a note in her diary that she had prayed in that way.

Two or three weeks later she received a letter from Don's mother in Canada. 'I felt constrained to pray for you specially today,' was the gist of what she said. 'You were so much in my mind I had to, even though I didn't know the reason.' Irene knew before she looked it up that it was the same date as the one she had marked.

Letters were the only tangible link she had with the outside world, but they kept her well-informed about the movements of her fellow-missionaries. David Day had suddenly been taken from prison and deported and had arrived in Hongkong, praising the Lord, on his birthday. The Saunders and their ten-year-old son had got through, too, the last missionaries to leave the province of Kansu. The Temples and one child . . . Beatrice Ebeling and two children . . . The Williamsons, the Simmonds, four Friedenshort Sisters. Mildred and Trudi, the two who had been her companions . . .

By the beginning of December the number of C.I.M.ers still in China was down to thirty-three, and five children. How long would it be before she and Don and the children would be moving towards the border – and freedom?

Christmas wasn't the happiest time she could remember, for the midnight visitor who secretly got in hadn't come to bring presents, but to take them. A wrist watch, a clock and a vest were missing – and the pocket-money Betty had so carefully saved. The little girl was quite upset because, as she explained, that money was sufficient to buy enough rice and vegetables to feed her for a week. 'She'd got it all worked out,' wrote Irene. 'She's caught the spirit of the times!'

But the tide of events was beginning to turn, though she did not know it, and a few days later she was called to the Police Station to meet Don. They could talk over their affairs together, she was told, provided they both spoke only in Chinese. He was to be moved, and she could prepare his clothes for travelling. Yes, she would be leaving shortly afterwards. No, they could not travel together.

The meeting, though it took place in the presence of the police, was a tremendous relief to them both, for neither had known what was happening to the other, nor how each had stood up to the strain. They looked at each other, the tall sensitive man and his short sturdy wife, and smiled. It was well with both of them. They had no opportunity to speak of anything but practical matters, but each saw the quiet confidence of faith in the other, and took heart. She handed over the clothes she had brought him and they parted, not knowing when they would meet again. The uppermost thought in their minds was the prospect of Irene and the three little children travelling unescorted across China, facing the mobs, finding their way through strange cities, down to the border . . .

'*Thus saith the Lord, I will go before you and make the crooked places straight,*' whispered Don.

The following day he was taken off with other prisoners, under armed guard, to Luhsien. It was on the road to Chungking. Perhaps she would catch up with him there, and they could travel on together. But the weeks passed, and although she was told to sell her possessions nothing further was said about her exit visa until the end of January. Then, suddenly, things began to move. She was told to take the first step of advertising her intended departure in the paper, and wondered if this would bring in a number of accusations and claims that would hold things up. On the contrary, the authorities hurried things on, as though eager now to get rid of her. 'You'll go under police escort to Luhsien. Here's your exit visa . . .' It looked as though she was a criminal, going that way, but the guard proved friendly, and she was glad he was there to protect them from the curious mobs who crowded in the towns they passed through.

Her hopes of travelling on from Luhsien with Don were disappointed, however, for she was not even allowed to see him there, only leave for him the two blank cheques and Ellison's instructions about travelling, in case he could use them. In spite of her protests that she could not travel alone with these three children all the way from Chungking to the border, she was hurried on.

Had she been permitted to see her husband in Luhsien she would have been so dismayed that her inward joy would have been threatened, for was he not part of her very being, and could she be unaffected by what happened to him? She did not know that he had entered a crucible of suffering greater than anything he had ever experienced before.

As it was, her main concern now was for the children, and getting them safely through to Hongkong with all the baggage they would need en route as well as when they arrived. How could she find the way through the crowds in Chungking to the inn? How could she obtain a passage on the down-river steamer, then change at Ichang, stay over in a strange inn, find her way to the station, change trains at Hankow, then at Canton, book in at strange inns again, hiring squabbling coolies at every point, all with a toddler in her arms and the other two both under ten, being swarmed by throngs of inquisitive people eager to touch these strange white children, perhaps tease them . . .?

Well, the Lord would provide. He would go before and make the crooked places straight. As they travelled towards Chungking, on the road with which she was fairly familiar, her thoughts went to fellow-missionaries who, as far as she knew, were still held in these provinces of the south and west. Very few of them left now. The four men under house-arrest in Kweiyang – she wondered if they had been freed. How wonderful it would be if one of them was in Chungking, waiting for a passage down-river, able to escort her. Oh, Lord – let it be so!

She arrived safely with the children and the luggage at the inn by the Yangtze in Chungking. There was no-one there whom she knew, but she made enquiries about booking a cabin on a steamer going to Ichang, and was told she could have one in the second-class section. That was a mercy, anyhow.

Then she realised there was a slight commotion at the front of the inn, and looking up she saw a figure that was certainly not Chinese. A foreigner had just arrived. She'd never met him before, but intuitively she knew . . .

'Mrs. Cunningham?' he asked when he saw her. 'I'm John Robinson, just arrived from Kweiyang. I thought they were going to put me in jail, but they let me have my exit visa instead – though they gave me the works first,' he added rather grimly. 'Well, I guess we're going in the same direction? We'll be able to travel together! I guess you'll be glad of a little help?'

Three weeks later they crossed the border. The welcome they received was ecstatic, but—

'Where's Don?' everyone was asking. No-one knew. Irene and the children were taken across to the rest-house on a little neighbouring island. There was nothing to be done now – just relax thankfully, and wait.

She'd only been there two days when Fred Keeble arrived, panting. His round face was rosy-red, his blue eyes blazing. It was a steep pull up that hill, but he was the bearer of news, and he wanted to get in with it first.

'Mrs. Cunningham! Mrs. Cunningham!' he called. 'Your husband's here!'

And there was Don! He was thin, his face gaunt, but he was smiling.

*   *   *

'It was terrible in Luhsien,' he told them all later. 'A man roped up was brought into the cell, thrown against the wall. He died and they just said, "He's dead." Just somebody less to feed! There was an epidemic. People died one after another. It was a testing time. I wondered if I'd ever reach Hongkong. God took me down and then raised me up again, as a testimony for Him. But it was His leading that Irene didn't see me there. I was sick, but the Lord strengthened me. I was only relieved when I was able to preach and to sing. The prisoners and the soldiers on guard heard – crept to their cell doors and listened.

'The men up top heard me, too – twenty or more of them. One of the men in cell No. One who'd been in three years, told me he heard me preach very clearly. He quoted John 3.16, which he had memorised from hearing me.

'The man in cell No. Two died. They put food inside the cell door, like feeding dogs. Then one night it wasn't there . . . They had trouble getting his body out, the door was so small. I trust he, too, heard the message and had an opportunity to believe before he died.

'Remarkable thing, there was a warder who was friendly to me. You could hear the rattle of chains when the warders took the prisoners out, and they not only threatened them but hit them, threw them on. But when they put the cuffs on me and I said, "They're a bit tight here," this fellow just took them off altogether.

'I only had my Bible the first three weeks then it was taken from me, but many times during those prison days the Word of God, His promises, came to mind and then the enemy would come in and test them. By faith I was able to lay hold. When in a small degree we have fellowship with the Lord in suffering, then we learn lessons we could never learn otherwise. But time and time again I must repeat, "*If it had not been the Lord who was on our side when men rose up against us; then they had swallowed us up quick . . . then the proud waters had gone over our soul. If it had not been the Lord who was on our side . . .*"

*   *   *

Very slowly now the names of those coming out of China were being crossed off the list that Arnold always kept by him. By the end of March 1952 there were still sixteen who had not got out, though all could be accounted for but one.

No word had come from Dr. Rupert Clarke for eight months, and all letters and cables sent to him had remained unanswered.

CHAPTER NINE

Tibetan Border

BEING A MEDICAL DOCTOR wasn't much use to Rupert Clarke now. He knew that unless something happened he couldn't live much longer. He'd had nothing to eat for three days and before that had been subsisting on the slimmest of diets, so since he was too weak and light-headed to stand or even sit, he'd taken to his bed.

Outside the walls of the deserted compound life continued as usual, coolies swinging along the dusty roads with their loads on carrying poles, peasants coming in to the market, a sprinkling of bold-eyed swashbuckling Tibetans among them. Dogs and hens scavenged around for what they could find. From the drill ground adjoining the back of the compound came the sounds of singing of patriotic songs, interspersed by sharp commands and the brisk marching of feet. If it was followed by the staccato snapping of rifle shots, he knew that probably someone was being executed.

Well, we've all got to die some time, and a bullet through the heart is a quicker way of going than starving by inches, which is what seemed to be happening in his case. He was faintly surprised that the Lord hadn't answered his prayer, as at other times, by providing food from some quarter or another. This time the days had passed emptily as usual. The only answer he had received had been the constant repetition in his own mind of Romans 8.28.

> '. . . *all things work together for good to them that love God, to them that are the called according to his purpose.*'

Not that he was exercising faith about that, or about anything else. It's easy to have faith in God when your body is well fed, well vitamised, but when everything is low it's another matter. His faith seemed to have failed. There was nothing left within himself that he could depend on. It was over to God now. Like Hudson Taylor had said, 'Hold the faithfulness of God. *If we believe not, yet He abideth faithful. He cannot deny himself.*' It was a comforting thought, because it made no demands on you any more. Rupert rolled over on his stomach, as he found that helped to ease the discomfort of hunger – there were no real pangs now, his body was so used to famishment – and gave up trying.

* * *

It was just over twenty years since an interest in China had first been kindled in him. He had been at quite a low ebb physically then, having just returned from a holiday in France with mumps and dysentery—a very ignominious condition for a young fellow embarking on a medical career. His grandmother, with whom he was staying, his parents being Army people and out of the country, helped to wile away the hours for him by reading aloud, and the book she chose was A THOUSAND MILES OF MIRACLES IN CHINA. It was a simply-written narrative of the harrowing experiences of a missionary family during the Boxer Rising of 1900, and had become a best-seller. It gripped him, as it had gripped countless others, and from that time he had a faint but persistent conviction that he himself was destined to go to China. The presence in the Christian Union in the Middlesex Hospital, where he was training, of Rob Pearce and Cecil Pedley, both of whom were already set to go there with the C.I.M., helped to deepen the impression. Not until he had graduated and was in his second year of hospital work, however, did he take the step of enquiring about application to the Mission, and even then did nothing further about the papers that were sent to him for some months. Perhaps he was waiting for something to give him a lead, but nothing occurred and eventually he decided that if he was going to do anything about China he'd better make a move. He must find out, once and for all, if it really was God's plan for him to go there.

He knew the formula for obtaining guidance, as outlined by George Müller and others – an open mind, the tenor of Scriptures, circumstances, prayer. He decided to try it for a week, praying and reading the Bible with this one aim in view.

He viewed his position objectively. He was in good health, had medical training which could be a help, no home responsibilities. The Lord's last commission to his disciples was clear enough, to go into all the world and make disciples. He prayed, 'Lord, let me know if it is Thy will for me to go to China.'

Within two days the matter was settled. All doubts were dissolved and indifference dispelled. No spectacular guidance was given, but he knew he should go forward. He filled in his application papers, went through the normal procedures and training, and set out for China in 1938.

The first few months were spent in language study, along with a group of other young fellows, including Jim Broomhall and David Bentley-Taylor from England and Arthur Mathews from Australia. 'The sons of the prophets' they were dubbed. Then they were dispersed, and he was on his way to Lanchow in the north-west.

It was the place to which he had always felt drawn, that springboard for Central Asia, for the Borden Memorial Hospital was there, needing doctors. The hospital compound with its low buildings straggling over the bare hillside on the banks of the Yellow River was the memorial to a wealthy young American whose short but ardent Christian life had made a deep impact on students of his own generation. Far and wide the fame of the hospital had spread through the years, and people travelled hundreds of miles to get to it for treatment – swarms of patient, quietly astute Chinese, tall arrogant Muslims, high-booted Turki with their little fez caps, diffident tribespeople conscious of being from minority groups, and Tibetans whose incessant mumbling of prayers and turning of prayer wheels in no way inhibited their enjoyment of life and ready indulgence in all forms of horseplay.

It was the Tibetans who captured Rupert's heart in a particular way, with their child-like buoyancy, and he talked to Jeanette about them. Jeanette's first job as a new missionary from South Africa had been to nurse him through typhoid, and their romance had started at that time. They'd had to wait quite a while to get married, simply because there was no-one in Lanchow and district qualified to perform the ceremony, and the problem was only solved when an Anglican clergyman, a member of the Mission, was flown in from Szechwan to do it. Now they were both working in the hospital, and both had noted the increasing number of Tibetans who were coming in from the rolling grasslands to get treatment.

Christian missionaries had always found these people particularly difficult to reach. Their nomadic way of life, their independence, above all their unquestioning allegiance to the Dalai Lama and his network of priests that spread out like a web from Lhasa over the whole country had proved formidable barriers, and the many efforts that had been made to bring them the Gospel had proved largely unsuccessful. But medical work had opened the way for the Evangel in so many places and among so many people, perhaps it would prove the key to the situation where the Tibetans in Tsinghai were concerned, too? So when, with the upsurge of missionary zeal among the Chinese, a group in the south-east, in affluent Chekiang, were prepared to come to the bleak Tibetan border in order to reach the Tibetans, the Clarkes were more than ready to co-operate in forming a medical clinic.

The clinic was opened on 5 July 1948 in the town of

Hwalung, south-east of Sining, the capital of Tsinghai. It was an occasion and a date that Rupert never forgot.

The opportunities were thrilling. With the help of bilingual local Chinese the medical work flourished. The clinic developed into a twenty-bed hospital. A Norwegian Pentecostal missionary in the district who had learned the Tibetan language could scarcely contain his joy at having provided for him audiences of twenty or thirty Tibetans at a time, instead of having to travel long journeys to reach two or three. The Communists took over in the following year quite peacefully, and all went on for the missionary team as before.

Then, in mid-1950, Rupert received an invitation to move further inland, to open medical work in a predominately Tibetan community.

At the same time Arthur Mathews, living in Lanchow, received an invitation from a little Chinese church to move into another remote region, also in Tsinghai province, near to an area where there were many Mongols.

Both men were ready to accept the challenge. For years Arthur had been praying for the Mongols – how could he draw back now, when at last the opportunity had come? For years Rupert had been praying for the Tibetans – how could he hold back when there was this opening to go still further among them?

Already the grip of Communism had tightened all over China. Everywhere missionaries, so far from being invited to extend their activities, were being asked to leave. Was it not remarkable that in this remote and backward province doors were actually opening?

Both men approached the Communist authorities with the invitations they had received, and asked permission to accept them. The response in each case was entirely different, but the outcome was the same.

Arthur Mathews was told he might go, and set off with his wife and child in the autumn of 1950 for Hwangyuan, thirty miles from Sining. When they arrived, covered with sleet and snow, saw the unpleasant accommodation allotted to them, sensed the fear behind the unfriendly welcome, they wondered if they had walked into a trap.

Rupert, in Hwalung, was sternly told he might *not* go. From that time the attitude of the Communist authorities hardened towards him. He suddenly realised he was in a net, and it was tightening.

After that, things rapidly took the course they had been taking in other parts of China. He was called repeatedly to the police station for questionings, all the members of his team had to fill in innumerable forms, the premises were searched unannounced at all times of the day and night. The harassment of the Christians was followed by the imprisonment of two of the Chinese assistants in the hospital. It was obvious that for the sake of others even more than themselves the missionaries must leave. They all applied for exit visas, the hospital was closed, and they prepared to depart.

They waited six months. Then one day in June they were told abruptly:

'You all go tomorrow!'

At last! All was hustle and bustle now, with the two missionary nurses, the Clarkes and the Norwegian Pentecostal couple paying off servants, hiring carts, packing, clearing up. It meant being up half the night but nobody minded that. Early in the morning the carts were driven into the compound, the loading up was under way, all were ready for departure when suddenly some police officials arrived.

'You must all go now – except you, Dr. Clarke! Someone has informed against you. You must stay. You must not leave this compound.'

What a morning! When the carts had all rumbled off, and he had had a last glimpse of Jeanette's anxious face looking back at him, six-months-old Humphrey in her arms, he went back alone into the empty rooms, bare, stripped, silent, and tried to prepare for the unknown. He found some bedding that had been left behind, there were stores of oil and rice and other foodstuffs, and fuel to cook by, so he'd be able to make meals for himself. There was nothing to do now but settle in as best he could, and wait. The angry roar of voices on the other side of the wall, in the drill ground, where an accusation meeting was being held, did not add to the comfort of his own situation.

Three days later one of the church members, a woman, came quietly into the compound and said to him, speaking very low:

'Dr. Clarke, they're going to have you up before the People's Court this afternoon. Agree to everything they accuse you of. By doing so you will be bowing to the will of the people. Otherwise you are against them, and it will go badly for you.'

When she left, Rupert's mind was in a turmoil. Agree to everything they accuse him of? If they charged him with anti-Marxist thinking he'd certainly acknowledge it, if they said he was arrogant and high-handed he'd be prepared to go along with them and acknowledge his own shortcomings, but what if they accused him of theft, or immorality, or political intrigue? How could he stand up and agree to a lie, even if by doing so he would save his own skin? How far could he go, what could he say?

It was at this point, when he was inwardly more confused than he had ever been before, that something sprang into his mind which stilled the inward storm as suddenly and completely as Christ stilled the storm on the lake of Galilee. Words that he had read time and time again unexpectedly became relevant.

> '*And when they bring you . . . unto magistrates and powers, take ye no thought how or what thing ye shall answer, or what ye shall say: For the Holy Ghost shall teach you in the same hour what ye ought to say.*'

With the command and the promise came the faith to believe. To his own surprise all anxiety went, and he was able to prepare quite calmly for what would probably be the outcome of the accusation meeting that awaited him. He spent the rest of the morning sprinkling DDT carefully into his underclothes in case he was sent to jail.

To begin with the accusation meeting went according to plan. The prisoner was marched along the dusty streets between armed guards to the open arena where a platform had been erected, and was pushed up onto it. A microphone had been set up and there were loud-speakers around, so when the National Anthem suddenly burst forth the two or three hundred people who had gathered sprang into action and sang lustily. Then the proceedings started in earnest. The official in charge, from his place on the platform, announced that the prisoner was an American spy. This was proved by the fact that people had died in his hospital after he had operated on them. Members of families were then brought forward to give evidence to this.

'Now what shall be done with him?' demanded the Communist official, turning to the crowd. 'Give your verdict!'

It was at this point that something went wrong. The time had come for the angry roar of voices, the vociferous demands for imprisonment or death, but on this occasion nothing happened. The crowd just stood silent, looking.

'What is your judgment?' asked the official again. Silence.

The two or three officials on the platform were in a quandary. They had a hurried consultation, then started picking on people in the crowd and asking:

'What do you think ought to be done to him?'

One of those they addressed was a Christian and a church leader. He was not the most whole-hearted spirit in the community, but as Rupert listened to his reply he felt it was inspired.

'I think he ought to be heavily fined and sent back to his own country.' Rupert, outwardly unmoved, applauded inwardly. There was plenty of money in the bank at Shanghai to pay a fine, and he would be delighted to be returned to his own country! The official was not satisfied, however.

'What do *you* think?' The question this time was addressed to the Muslim assistant mayor.

'Better put him in prison!'

'And you?' This time it was the Chinese assistant mayor who had to answer up.

He had been owing Rupert some money for a very long time.

'Kill him!' he shouted.

In the end Rupert was sent to jail pending instructions from the capital as to what was to be done with him.

There were forty other prisoners already in the cell into which he was pushed. It was about twelve feet square, so it was not easy to get in, nor easy to find a place to sit, either. But the other prisoners, mainly Muslims, were quite friendly, and moved up to make room for him. One more or less made little difference, anyhow. There was only room to sit, huddled up, not to lie down, and the diet was coarse bread and water twice a day. Some of the inmates had been on it for months.

Such conditions are dispiriting. No-one was inclined to talk much, and though Rupert tried from time to time to preach the Gospel, he got little response, except a shout from the guard who yelled to stop conversation if it went on too long. It was all the more surprising and heartening, therefore, to hear suddenly a voice uplifted in a neighbouring cell, singing rather huskily:

> 'The Lord gives me peace,
>   The peace that the Lord gives
>   Is out of this world,
>   And no man can take it away.'

He learned afterwards that the singer was known to Arthur Mathews, and had been sentenced to three months' imprisonment for refusing to co-operate with the authorities.

When the fourth day of his imprisonment dawned, Rupert remembered the date. It was 5 July, the anniversary of the opening of the clinic. 'Lord,' he prayed silently, huddled up in the cell. 'It's an anniversary – please give me a nice present!' He didn't know what to expect, but somehow he believed the Lord had heard and taken note, so he wasn't altogether surprised when, a few hours later, he was called out of the cell and brought before the chief official.

'We've had no word about you from the capital yet,' he was told. 'So we're sending you back to your compound. On no account must you leave it without permission. We're appointing an old man to do your shopping for you.'

Back to the deserted compound, with a clean bed on which to stretch himself, food to cook, his Bible and a few books! It was a very, very good anniversary present!

A fortnight later he received two telegrams. One was from Jeanette, saying she had obtained a passage to South Africa. The other was from the British Government official in Peking, asking after his welfare. He received no more communications from the outside world after that, nor was he allowed to send any.

The weeks passed, and the months passed. He measured the compound and set himself to walk ten *li* each day, and thirty *li* once a week, to keep fit. Especially he wanted to be fit enough for the journey he hoped one day he would take to Sining. It was a long, hard journey over mountains, and he knew he couldn't expect the Communists to supply him with an animal – he'd have to walk, for sure, though the guards might be mounted, and he'd have to keep up with them! Apart from that self-imposed exercise there was plenty to keep him active, what with cleaning and cooking and washing his clothes. In addition to his Bible, his library consisted of an American medical book, a commentary on John's Gospel, and some novels by Walter Scott, John Buchan, and *East Lynne* by Mrs. Henry Wood. He read them over and over again, for the days were empty of human companionship except when one of the Christians slipped in for a brief chat, or the Communists came along to talk the party line. They failed to win him over but he was quite glad to see them all the same. It helped to break the silence and the monotony.

On Christmas Day, to his great surprise, he had a string of visitors. The local Christians came to see him, one by one, throughout the day.

'But isn't it dangerous for you to do this?' he asked. 'If you're seen . . .'

'Not really,' was the answer. ' "They" seem to be keeping Christmas, too, in their own way. They're all together at the Police Station. It's very cold out, after all.'

'By the way, you know there were a few Tibetans at Labrang who were secret believers? Well, they're meeting quite openly together for worship and prayer now. The Communists have closed the lamaseries and set the lamas to work, so no-one's afraid of them any more!'

Altogether, it was quite a good Christmas after all, thought Rupert.

His money was running low by this time, and the sixth chapter of Matthew's Gospel contained passages to which he referred time and time again.

'Lord,' he prayed, pointing to verse thirty-three, 'I'm here because I sought first your Kingdom, your righteousness.' As far as he knew, he was the only C.I.M. missionary left in China now – maybe the only white man, he thought sometimes. 'Here is your promise – that you'd supply what I needed. Lord, I'm nearly at the end of my food supply now. I'm looking to you.'

Shortly after that a little boy came on to the compound. He recognised the child. His father was a lapsed church member.

'My father's sent me to ask how you're off for food, Dr. Clarke,' said the little boy.

'Well, I've got enough for one more meal,' said Rupert honestly.

'Don't worry – my father will bring you some.'

Half an hour later another little boy arrived. His father also was a lapsed church member. The same question was asked, the same answer given. That afternoon the two men arrived separately, each bringing food.

'Put your heart at rest, Dr. Clarke,' they said. 'Whatever the Communists do, we won't let you starve.'

They were as good as their word. Every day food was smuggled in, usually by the two little boys. The petition 'Give us this day our daily bread' took on a new significance, for the food that was brought was usually baked bread. After about six weeks even that supply failed, however, for the Communists put an armed guard at the gate of the compound, and no-one could come in unnoticed any more.

There was just one way left to obtain food now, and Rupert considered it carefully. He knew that the hospital food store was not properly sealed. It was frozen over, but by a little judicious melting it could be opened, and he could get in and take what he needed. No moral scruples deterred him. The food belonged to his Mission, and he had a perfect right to it. He hesitated because he realised what would happen if he were found by the Communists to have taken it. He could see in his mind's eye the headlines blazoned in newspapers all over north-west China – 'Mission doctor steals hospital food!' It was just the sort of incident that would make fine copy to bring the Mission and all that it stood for into disrepute.

Even if you were alone, and no-one would know about it, you didn't let the side down. So Rupert refrained, though he was getting very hungry, and a verse from the book of Proverbs clinched the matter for him.

> *'Trust in the Lord with all thine heart;*
> *and lean not to thine own understanding.'*

'Thine own understanding.' The Chinese rendering implied human cleverness, slickness. He turned his eyes and his thoughts away from that easily opened lock, made some soup with the remains of a half-rotten cabbage, and took to his bed. He was through. There was nothing else he could do. He was too exhausted to pray, to exercise faith, far less to praise.

'Hold the faithfulness of God.' It was over to Him now.

*   *   *

Brisk footsteps crossed the compound, the bedroom door was flung open, and the Communist cadre exclaimed contemptuously:

'What are you doing, lying in bed in the middle of the day! Why aren't you up and about? Why aren't you doing your exercise?'

Rupert rolled over and tried to sit up in a respectful attitude.

'Well you see I haven't had anything to eat for three days,' he explained reasonably. 'So I'm too weak to walk about now. I fall over. It's safer lying here.'

'Why haven't you eaten for three days?'

'I haven't any food left.'

The cadre took a quick look round, then said, 'You must write a report to the Chief of Police. I'll take it to him.' Rupert laboriously wrote a few lines on a sheet of paper, the cadre took the paper and departed.

An hour or so later a young Communist soldier slipped quietly into the room and handed Rupert some bread. 'Don't tell anyone I've brought this,' he whispered. 'They're going to give you an allowance of food from tomorrow, but I didn't want you to go through the night hungry.' There were human hearts beating under some of those jackets, after all!

The turn of the tide had come. Food was supplied daily, but Rupert's strength returned very slowly, and it was not long before it was decided to send him to Sining. They didn't want a sick foreigner on their hands – let the authorities in Sining be responsible for him.

An animal and an armed guard were provided for the journey, but as Rupert was obviously too weak to walk it was he who had the mount, the guard walking beside him. And instead of being taken to the jail, as he had expected, he noticed he was being led along the familiar road leading to the C.I.M. compound. Not until he got inside, however, did he know that he was not, after all, the only missionary left in China for there, looking at him with an expression of incredulity that quickly changed to delight, was Seepy.

CHAPTER TEN

Invisible Provider

CLARENCE PREEDY, whose initials provided him with the convenient nickname of Seepy, had had an unusually eventful career, inextricably bound up with the China Inland Mission, since he had been born into it. He had been a pupil in Chefoo, it's school for missionaries' children in North China, got some clerical training and experience in England, then sailed again for China in the 1930s, for his was a missionary calling, like his parents. The country was already threatened by the Japanese invasion, and by the time he'd completed his first term of service he had been in occupied territory for four years, and had seen and heard quite enough of the misery of the vanquished. It was with a sense of intense relief that he and his wife (he was married by this time) saw the shores of China disappearing beyond the horizon of the open sea as they set off for Manila on the first stage of their journey to the U.S.A. A period for renewal and refreshment at home was just what was needed to prepare them for another term of overseas missionary work, and they were looking forward to it eagerly – and to showing off their two little daughters to admiring relatives who had never yet seen them.

Their ship steamed slowly into the far-famed Manila harbour, with its small palm-fringed islands and sandy beaches, late one Sunday evening early in December 1941. It was a scene of indescribable beauty in the vivid glory of the setting sun, and a sense of peace and well-being suffused them as they settled down to sleep that night.

The next morning their tranquillity was completely shattered.

They were awakened with the news that without any warning the Japanese had bombed the U.S. naval base of Pearl Harbour in the Hawaiian Islands, immobilising their defences, and laying the whole of South-East Asia open to invasion. Japan had entered the war against the Allies. It would only be a matter of days before Manila was occupied, and there was no hope of getting away before it happened. The Preedy family found themselves stranded in a strange city where they knew no-one, completely cut off from all their normal sources of supply and branded as enemy nationals by the conquering Japanese.

They expected to be interned, along with others of their own nationalities, but to their consternation were not admitted. 'No sick people, and no babies under one year need report at the camp,' they were told by the Japanese officer in charge. The authorities washed their hands of such incumbrances without making any suggestion as to how they were to survive. As enemy nationals the Preedys were not allowed to work for a living, nor buy food with their travellers' cheques, since American money was forbidden currency. Humanly speaking, they were faced with the prospect of either dying of starvation or begging on the streets.

'This is a test of faith,' said Clarence. When they joined the China Inland Mission they had both asserted that their faith was in God, not in any human organisation, and now they were to prove it. Their experiences ranged from living rent-free in a comfortable, fully-furnished bungalow to sitting beside all their baggage in the street, surrounded by curious bystanders, not knowing where to go. Yet they were confident that God would provide for them, and provide for them He did, in many unexpected and varied ways. The saga of their three and a half years in Manila was a continuous story of faith exercised and rewarded, as through other missionaries, Filipino and Chinese Christians and kind-hearted Spaniards help came, sometimes in the very nick of time.

Their worst experiences, strangely enough, were when the tide of the war had turned, and the American forces were preparing to land in the Philippines. The family had been increased by this time. Baby Raymond was being looked after in one home, Roberta who had been seriously ill in another, the two little girls in yet another, while Clarence was living in a church some distance away. With his red armband designating him as an enemy alien, he visited his family only once a week, for fear of drawing attention to the kind friends who were providing the hospitality.

Then the bombing started. General McArthur was fulfilling his promise given when he had been forced out of the Philippines three years earlier. 'I shall return,' he had said, and in one sense the bombings were welcomed, as it meant deliverance from the Japanese invaders was on the way. But it was obviously a case of things getting worse before they could get better, and the city began to be in turmoil, with people fleeing to the country, food becoming scarce, and prices soaring. The family fostering Raymond took him away with them to the north of Luzon Island, and after a further upheaval Clarence and Roberta found themselves at one end of the space above a ramshackle garage, curtained and screened off from the public eye by an old mosquito net. In these unlikely surroundings Clarence contrived to fit up a desk so that he could use his time profitably in Bible study.

As it happened, it was during this period that they both went without food of any sort for three days – the only time in the whole three and a half years that they were really destitute. 'Praise the Lord the girls are being looked after!' they said. It would have been hard to have the children with them, scenting the delicious odours rising up from a neighbour's kitchen below, and having nothing to give them to eat. As it was, they regaled themselves by browsing over some old recipes, well-illustrated, of chocolate cakes, steaming soups, and other delicacies, while praying that the Lord would supply them with something more physically nourishing.

The answer to their prayers on this occasion came in a very simple and practical way. The same thought occurred to them simultaneously. Sell something and get some money! That old blanket! These trinkets – they should fetch something! Why hadn't they thought of it before?

They broke their fast that day, and after that they always had enough to eat.

Meanwhile, the Japanese were slowly retreating, commandeering every kind of vehicle they could lay hands on, burning buildings and blowing up military stores and dumps as they went. The fighting was on now, and for a day or two the Preedys found themselves in a sort of no-man's-land, with shells landing from both sides. But the arrival of a Spanish general to see the family from whom he had been separated for three years made it evident which side was gaining ground now. The wave of war passed over, the civilians who had been cowering in their air-raid shelters emerged, and a flood of refugees poured back into the city to escape the wholesale slaughter and destruction the Japanese were wreaking as they withdrew.

The Preedys were caught up in this flood of humanity, for the home in which the two little girls were staying was suddenly inundated with friends and relatives, and there was no longer any room for the destitute white family. Clarence had been trying in vain to get in touch with the American authorities, but was unable to do so. Conditions were chaotic, and only those duly registered in the internment camps were being dealt with. He was nearly at his wits' end when he bumped into a Chinese doctor whom he had met once before, at a prayer meeting. In the course of their ensuing conversation the doctor asked how he was getting on, now that the Americans had arrived.

'Nowhere to stay!' he exclaimed when Clarence told

him. 'Come and stay with me – bring your family today!' So the Englishman and his American wife made their way across the liberated city, pushing their dilapidated bundles on an old railway hand-truck and a broken-down pram, to receive the warm-hearted hospitality of a Chinese Christian family. It was a long time before they began to reap the full benefits of liberation.

If only they could get into that internment camp, where the processes for repatriation started! Another apparently chance meeting expedited matters. This time it was with Edwin Orr, Chaplain of the United States Armed Forces. He did not hesitate to take up their case and things started moving quickly after that. Within a week of entering the internment camp Roberta and the children were on their way to the States at last, while Clarence waited behind for the missing member of the family.

The over-riding anxiety during these weeks had been for little Raymond, and the news that eventually came through Army Intelligence Headquarters that the whole party in which the family fostering him had journeyed had been captured and interned by the Japanese was alarming. The worst could be anticipated, for everything was in complete disarray now, and who would be concerned for one little white baby in the midst of it all?

Probably at no other time was any member of the Preedy family prayed for with such intensity and by so many, both in Manila and the U.S.A., as that little boy.

Weeks passed. No news.

Then one Sunday, on his way to church, Clarence was almost knocked down by a jeep which jerked to a standstill right in front of him. Out jumped an American soldier.

'Just read this message and sign your name at the bottom, will you?' he said, thrusting a sheet of paper before Clarence. On it were simply written the words:

YOUR SON ARTHUR RAYMOND AND PARTY ARE SAFE AND WELL SOMEWHERE IN LUZON.

Clarence Preedy and his little son eventually landed in Seattle on 17 August 1945, three days after Japan had surrendered unconditionally to the Allies. The Preedy family was reunited at last. They were quite ready for furlough!

* * *

Some like it tough, they say. It would not have been surprising if, after some ten years of particularly harrowing experiences, the Preedys had decided to accept a job in the U.S.A. and settle down. They had an unusual story to tell, with some remarkable evidences of God's intervention and provision. Clarence, in fact, wrote a cheerful little book about those three and a half years in Manila, the culmination of his first period of missionary service. There were plenty of openings for him to preach and teach, and inspire others by what he had to tell. However, he had no doubt as to where he ought to go. As a soldier of Jesus Christ all he wanted was to be where his Captain sent him, and he knew that that place was back in China now. He arrived there with his family some time in the late 1940s, ready for another term of service, and was asked to go to Sining, provincial capital of Tsinghai, on the Tibetan border. With his clerical experience he would be able to help fellow-missionaries further inland, as a sort of business manager at a supply base with Roberta in charge of the Mission home.

They were there when the Communists took over. They saw the usual changes, with restrictions increasing, interrogations, arrests, accusations, executions, and finally the pressure put on local Christians because of the presence of western missionaries, which had resulted in the Mission's order to withdraw. Roberta, along with others from the province, had left in June 1951 and now, ten months later, he was still here, having seen several other missionaries safely through the city and on their way out to freedom. For the last three months, in the bitter cold of winter, he had been alone, and the deepest impression that had been made on him through that time had been, not so much his own isolation and the atmosphere of fear brooding over the city, as the sovereignty of God. Hour after hour he had spent, wrapped in his wadded clothes, sitting up on the verandah to take advantage of the brilliant north China sunshine, leaning against the wall with ruler and pencil in his hand, reading through *The Reformed Doctrine of Predestination,* underlining words and sentences, turning the pages of his Bible to check this and that. There had been times when he had been completely oblivious to the sights and sounds around him, so absorbed had he been with his subject.

> 'Our God is in the heavens: He hath done whatsoever He hath pleased...'

His heart had exulted at the realisation that the God in the heavens was His God – the same God who had mystically revealed His plans to His prophets of old. Who had worked and was still working through the history of mankind.

> 'Immortal, invisible, God only wise,
>   In light inaccessible, hid from our eyes,
>   Most blessed, most glorious, the Ancient of days...'

His very soul seemed to soar in worship, above the birds circling overhead, higher than the barren mountains on the horizon. God ruled. Seepy was sure about that.

'Our times are in Thy hands'. The words came again and again to reassure him, as they had been coming to many others of his fellow-missionaries in various parts of China. At the appointed hour deliverance would come, and nothing could prevent it. What God had planned would come to pass, and nothing could prevent it!

*   *   *

Not that he was able always to remain in a position of rejoicing faith. There were times when he was acutely conscious of his loneliness, and March was a particularly difficult month, with accusation meetings in full spate in the city, and he wondered if his turn would come to face a howling mob. When he recorded briefly in his diary 'Typhoon raging', he hadn't been referring to the weather. Rumours had reached him of what he was likely to be accused of, and by whom, and the news had been disturbing. On April 8 he read in the Psalms:

> '*But mine enemies are lively, and they are strong; and they that hate me wrongfully are multiplied.*
>
> *They also that render evil for good are mine adversaries;*
>
> *because I follow the thing that good is.*
>
> *All that hate me whisper together against me; against me do they devise my hurt.*
>
> *Yea, mine own familiar friend, in whom I trusted, which did eat of my bread, hath lifted up his heel against me.*'

He knew just how the psalmist had felt when he wrote those words.

He had run short of food at the end of March, as not infrequently happened when the time drew near to draw the allowance granted to him, and it had been comforting to receive a parcel containing some home-made cake and biscuits from Arthur and Wilda Mathews in the neighbouring town. It wasn't just the food, it was the sense of fellowship that had been so heartening. The strain of uncertainty and apprehension was intensified by the loneliness. If only he had a companion!

*   *   *

Over a rough road through the mountains, coming towards Sining, was a mule bearing an emaciated man, an armed Communist soldier walking alongside. They entered the city on April 10, the eve of Good Friday. The only entry in Seepy's diary that day was simply, 'RUPERT arrived'.

*   *   *

For Rupert it was a Rip Van Winkle-like experience to arrive in Sining and once more be in touch with the Mission – or what was left of it in China. He was too weakened physically to take very much interest in anything at first, however. 'He looks like Pharaoh's second batch of kine' was the way Seepy described his appearance when he wrote to the Mathews to tell them of his arrival. The most important thing to do was to get a cable off to H.Q., and since Rupert did not know his wife's address in South Africa and there was no money to waste, the cable was short but concise.

INFORM JEANETTE   ARRIVED SINING   MAILLESS SEVEN
MONTHS   LOVINGLY   RUPERT

After that Rupert was content to take things easily, and listened quietly while Seepy brought him up-to-date with events.

'Less than twenty C.I.M.ers left in China now. We two and the Mathews are the only ones up here in the north-west. The Mathews have been having a pretty grim time of it. They walked into trouble when they got to Hwang-yuan, right from the start. Instead of having the Mission house as they expected, they found themselves with only a kitchen and a bedroom – had to go out and walk across the compound and up a flight of stairs to get to the bed-room. Unheated, of course. Imagine Wilda carrying that baby girl across the courtyard in the snow after her bath, and leaving her up in that icy bedroom! Eventually they gave it up – just live and sleep in the kitchen now.

'They're having their financial difficulties too, like me. Worse, in a way – Arthur has to go and plead for their allowance every time, and then he's kept waiting around outside the office for hours on end, like a beggar.

'No, no help from the church – same as here, frightened to death to have anything to do with us. There are always the faithful individuals, though – they have a young Chinese fellow who came up here from south of Shanghai to do missionary work. He lives by faith, partly supported by his church down south. He's been a tower of strength to them. A White Russian Christian, too, married to a Chinese. Suppose he knows what it feels like, being a stranger in a strange land!

'Arthur was accused on five counts by a woman in Changyeh, where he was earlier. He signed a confession admitting all of them - a masterpiece of grovelling that had us howling with laughter when we read it. But the Commies, of course, took it seriously. He was accused of:

'Standing on a table belonging to the church. (It was rickety, and the church didn't want it.)

'Misusing a memorial plaque.

'Locking the kitchen door of the church.

'Closing the school at Changyeh. (These in accordance with the church and school's wishes.)

'Killing a dog. (The dog was a stray, and the deacon asked him to kill it.)

'The matter was finally solved by payment of U.S. $135 to the lady who had been offended!

'But you never know what else may be brewing – they may come up with something more serious next time.'

'Like murder - that's what they had against me.' Rupert was reminded. 'Some of my patients had died . . .'

'Jeanette had to face a charge when she got to Lanchow - did you know about that? Someone she'd dismissed from the hospital for misconduct years ago took advantage of the opportunity to get her own back. Jeanette got let off with a fine which the Mission paid, of course, so it wasn't too bad, though it was tense at the time.

'Everyone's out of Kansu province now, thank God. Strange thing - the folk in Ningsia province had no difficulties at all. They were quite reluctant to leave—couldn't think what all the fuss was about!'

Gradually Rupert got a picture of the situation. Mission Headquarters were out of China now, in Hongkong. J.R.S. had retired. Bishop Houghton, so often ill, had resigned. Letters from H.Q. were very circumspect, mainly news about individuals, with only veiled intimations that the Mission was launching out into other countries of South-East Asia. The less said the better about that, as long as there were still some of its members held in Communist China!

'The Goulds are still in Shanghai, working for Butterfield and Swire. Don't know what we should have done without them. They keep the cash flowing this way, though they can't do anything about it being frozen when it gets here. But they write frequently, enclose stamps in their letters, send parcels from time to time. Most missionaries are away from Shanghai by this time and other foreigners too, including the clergy – so Harry is now Dean of the Cathedral! Elizabeth's descriptions of him in his robes . . .! They're both having plenty of opportunities for Bible classes, preaching, and so on. Things are much easier in the big cities – it's these remote places where the pressure is hardest.'

Such news as was available about the state of the churches varied. In all places there was pressure on the Christians to vilify the missionaries. The usual pattern had been to speak out against missionaries who were long since dead, or had left the country and who therefore would not be affected by what was said. But this had been unacceptable. They must speak against those who were still alive, and in the locality! Church members had then mentioned trivial and innocuous matters, in some cases no accusations had been made. Henry Guinness in Nanking had been brought up for trial, and not one person had been found to speak against him! But the pressure was on, and some of the most respected and reliable Christian leaders had been reported as having made virulent verbal attacks against their erst-while friends and colleagues. The picture was not a bright one, though lit up by courageous and triumphant evidences of undying faith and loyalty by individuals, like the adopted son of an elderly missionary, who went to his execution with shining face, singing hymns, or the old Mission employee who, instead of launching forth into an expected tirade at an accusation meeting, related publicly all the help he had received through the years from the missionaries he had served. And many, many young people, members of the I.V.F., had been executed or sent to labour camps for their faith.

The two men settled down to a simple routine within the limitations of the compound wall. Cooking, cleaning, digging, planting vegetables, writing carefully worded letters, reading, praying together. For each the indefinable burden of loneliness was lifted, and they were thankful to be spared the lot of the Roman Catholic Fathers who had been imprisoned in the city jail the day after Easter. In the middle of May Rupert received a batch of letters, the first he had had for eight months, and the fairly regular delivery of mail every ten days kept them in touch with the outside world. They learned, among other things, that they were now among the only eight members of the Mission still remaining in China.

In thickly populated Hunan province south of the Yangtze Dr. and Mrs. Witt and Mr. and Mrs. Hollenweger, German missionaries, had been applying for exit visas as unsuccessfully as themselves. Sincere pleas that the two wives, at least, might be permitted to go, since both were ill, had met with stern refusals. In Tsinghai province, bordering the Tibetan grasslands, there were themselves and the Mathews with little Lilah. Everyone else had got away.

During those later months of 1952 the most memorable experiences of the four of them in Tsinghai were connected with mankind's basic need – food. The subject was constantly in their minds for the reason that the monthly allowance granted to them by the local authorities was quite insufficient for their needs. It was barely enough from April to September, but then it was cut by about half, and they knew they could barely survive on it. For the Mathews, particularly, the test was intensified, because of the constant delays in drawing even the little that was allowed them. Time and time again they got on their knees, Bibles opened before them at the sixth chapter of Matthew's Gospel, to remind their Heavenly Father of His promises. They told no-one but Him of their need. Time and time again, when they were almost at their last resources, provision came.

They were out of salt. You have to be out of salt, to have none at all, to know how much you depend on it. The White Russian Christian, who sold salt on his stall, suddenly presented them with half a basket full of it.

They had been without meat for weeks, and other stores were very low. A knock came at the door one evening. The White Russian's little girl was there, with ten pounds of meat for them.

They had to cut their milk order for several weeks – but during that time the milk was richer than ever before, and had to be watered down.

A deaf old Tibetan woman, so weak she had to crawl up the steps to their door, arrived one day with six little steamed breads.

A parcel arrived from the Goulds in Shanghai – something was sent from Hongkong . . . So it went on, and for the two men in Sining also. They were reduced to a diet of beans at one stage, when the old Muslim woman who in the past had supplied them with milk arrived at the compound. She had a big sack with her, and when the door opened in response to her knock she staggered in with it, emptied the contents into a bin, and departed. Seepy looked into the bin and saw with amazement that it was full of potatoes.

'Only God could have made her do that!' he told Rupert. 'She'd never have been willing otherwise!'

On another occasion, when both food and money were at an end, they were walking round the yard, taking their daily exercise, when they noticed a little cardboard bundle lying on the ground. They were familiar with every stone, every tuft of weed in the ground by that time, and spotted it almost simultaneously. Carefully they opened it to see what it contained.

It was a roll of banknotes.

They never learned how that bundle got there. Rupert favoured the idea that it had fallen from the pocket of one of the policemen who prowled around on the flat roofs, keeping an eye on them. Seepy was of the opinion that a hawk, having swooped down on to a food stall and picked it up in mistake for meat, had discarded it in disgust in mid-air. What they were both agreed on, however, was that by whatever means it had come, the source of the supply was their Father in heaven, who had heard their cry and once more fulfilled His promise to provide for their need.

As the months of 1952 slipped into the past and Christmas drew near, Rupert, with his tendency to note anniversaries, reviewed the situation as it related to the pantry. They had an adequate supply of beans, and with the potatoes the old Muslim had brought they were not badly off, but he felt, nevertheless, that it would make rather poor fare with which to celebrate Christmas. He decided to pray about it, explaining to the Lord that he wasn't really asking for something that they needed, since what they had in hand was enough – but could He see His way to grant something extra, as a favour? A sort of Christmas present?

A short time later a man he had known in the past came in from the street.

'I happened to be passing and remembered I owed you some money,' he said. He had owed it for so long, Rupert had forgotten about it. 'So I thought I'd come right in and repay you now.'

'Oh, thank you,' said Rupert calmly. He was very good at concealing his feelings, though his secret 'Thank you' to God was quite uninhibited. Then he lost no time in buying sugar, flour, raisins and various other delicacies. He did some baking to prepare for the festive season, and since he had developed quite a knack in cooking, made a fruit cake for the Mathews, and sent it off post-haste that it might be in time for Christmas.

Meanwhile, the Mathews had had an unexpected windfall, the local authorities having suddenly released an unprecedented amount of money, so Wilda made fudge and various kinds of biscuits, and despatched a parcel to Sining.

Seepy, somewhat distressed at being the only one who was not sending off a present, suddenly remembered something. He had a pound of coffee which he had bought a year or two earlier, and was keeping for a special occasion. This should be the occasion! He packed it up and mailed it to the Mathews. They had the coffee-pot out again, the first time for a year or more, on Christmas morning.

It was, in fact, one of the happiest Christmases they had in China. They had managed to preserve a little rosebush with leaves on it, so that made a Christmas tree. Lilah, who had been ill and at death's door in the summer, was strong and healthy now, a little girl eager to know if Santa Claus would come. Hand-made cloth toys, carefully ironed ribbons, hankies, booklets, transfers, all ingeniously contrived out of who-knows-what, convinced her that he had arrived. In the middle of the morning a knock at the door revealed a kindly Chinese friend with sweets and a celluloid man for her. Then Ben, the young Chinese evangelist, turned up with a toy with a heavy bottom that you couldn't knock over. Their little girl was as happy as a little girl could be, and what more could parents desire?

But there was something else that had brought an overwhelming relief to their minds, releasing the tension in which they had been living for months. On Christmas Eve, the very day before Christmas, the spy who had been living on the compound, who had watched their every movement, reported on their activities, noted who went to visit them and reported it, the Judas who had turned against them, departed.

Timothy was his name, and he had come, like Ben, sent by a church in the south to do evangelistic work on the border. The two young fellows had lived together for over a year, and all had gone well until they were taken off, separately, to accusation meetings in Sining. As everyone knew, the aim of the long indoctrination they would undergo would be that they would declare themselves wholly in favour of the Communist regime, then so criticise others, especially the missionaries, that a criminal charge could be brought against them.

Those meetings proved a watershed in the lives of the two young men. Ben returned from them unscathed. The Lord had stood with him and helped him, he said, and his 'criticism' of the missionaries had been only what was already known. The other, Timothy, returned a changed man. His face was against his former friends, and hard-eyed he remained on the church compound, living in the room above the one the Mathews occupied, watching . . . The police forbade anyone on the compound to speak to them on pain of going to prison, and he was there to see if anyone disobeyed the order.

From that time, in May, the Mathews had lived in virtual isolation, their neighbours passing them with averted faces, those who wished to befriend them doing so secretly, knowing the risk they took.

And now Timothy had gone. It did not seem possible, but the evidence was clear. He had boarded the bus for Sining, taking his belongings with him. 'He's gone! He's on the way to Sining! He's not coming back!'

It was because he was out of the way that they were

able to receive the crowning joy of Christmas. The pastor of the church, who had been afraid to come near them for months, arrived at their door in the evening, smiling his greetings.

'Happy Holy Birthday! Happy Holy Birthday!' he said. Then he added, 'The church is packed! We're having a special Christmas service, and many, many people have come in. They're there now, singing. We're going to tell them how the Saviour came to earth. I knew you'd be glad to know. Pray for us! Holy Happy Birthday!' and he departed.

Arthur and Wilda sat back in their chairs, looked at each other quietly, and smiled. This was what really mattered – that the Evangel was still being proclaimed, and that Christ's people were proclaiming it. Yes, it had been a happy Christmas! It was rounded off the following day by the arrival of a parcel from an anonymous well-wisher in Switzerland, containing books, a toy wrist watch that wound up, colour book and crayons, and three bars of chocolate. It came via the Post Office. 'We don't know who sent it, or how it got through.'

Less than a week later the Bamboo Curtain lifted again, as Dr. and Mrs. Witt and Mr. and Mrs. Hollenwager crossed the border on New Year's Day. Arnold Lea, in the Mission's new Headquarters in Singapore from which workers were streaming out to the countries of South-East Asia and Japan in ever-increasing numbers, drew out the large sheet of paper on which were typed the names of those still in China in early 1951. Triumphantly he dashed his pencil through four more names, then made another entry at the bottom of the page, the first he had made since 22 May 1952, when he recorded eight still left in China.

Jan 1953 ... 4.

All were in Tsinghai, on the Tibetan border.

CHAPTER ELEVEN

Countdown to Zero

THE DAYS PASSED so uneventfully on the C.I.M. compound in Sining, those early months of 1953, that the entries in Seepy's diary were confined almost exclusively to the particular Scriptures that had impressed him in his daily readings. The routine of keeping alive and warm in the bitter cold of winter on the high Tibetan plateau was only broken by periodical calls for repetitive questionings at the Police Station, not worth recording. The Word of God was different. As he and Rupert studied it, alone or together, it had an animating effect upon their spirits which could range, unhindered by time or circumstances, back into the history of mankind or forward into the glowing glory of Eternity. It kept hope alive, nourished patience, and provided a never-failing escape from the monotony of life in the confined compound.

One day in March, however, the monotony was broken by an event both human and visible. About noon the gate of the compound was opened, and in came a coolie carrying some very worse-for-wear luggage, followed by a woman leading a child by the hand. They were dressed in Chinese clothes, but one glance told him they were not Chinese. Wilda Mathews and her little girl stood there.

'Why, it's Wilda!' he exclaimed, hastening forward to meet her. Two and a half years had passed since last he saw her, and he noticed how thin she had become. Then he saw little Lilah, plump and healthy, a balloon dangling from one end of the chopstick she clutched in her hand, and smiled. Whatever privations the parents had suffered, their little girl had been spared. 'You've really got here this time!'

Over a month ago he had heard they were coming, then at the last minute, just when they were dressed and ready to get on the bus, they had been held up. It was the sixth time the cat-and-mouse game had been played, but as Wilda said:

'We were neither of us upset – been fooled too often, I guess! And before long we felt it was the Lord's overruling. I was hoping we could both leave together, but one morning, after I'd been pleading with the Lord that it might be so, I was confronted with Romans 9.21. "*Who art thou that repliest against God? Hath not the Potter power over the clay?*" So I faced it squarely. All I could do was to bow my heart and head and say, "not my will, but Thine be done". It's a comfort to be able to leave it all with Him.

'Yes, they gave me my exit visa and travel permit,' she went on, in answer to the all-important question. 'They told me they were letting me go because I've got no more money, but they'd keep Arthur behind because there were serious charges against him – against Dr. Clarke, too. The Regime knows how to deal with criminals, they said.'

There was little doubt as to what charge would be brought against Rupert. Murder! It was simple enough to bring a case against a doctor, for what doctor has never had patients who have eventually died? But no-one knew what they were holding against Arthur.

As for Seepy, it seemed that they were finished with him. No charges were brought against him, after all. He could start the usual procedures for obtaining an exit visa they told him. Advertise in the papers, find someone to stand guarantor, fill in the forms, buy your ticket and depart! Yes, you may escort Mrs. Mathews and the child . . .

They didn't get rid of him quite so easily as that, though. He still took his responsibilities as business manager seriously, and there were one or two things he wanted to know. He wrote them down to ensure they were not overlooked. When eventually he boarded the bus that would take them to Lanchow on the first stage of the long journey south, he knew that Rupert would be allowed to go to market to buy his vegetables, that he would hold the keys and the bank-book, and could draw the monthly allowance for Arthur as well as himself. And since Harry Gould in Shanghai had discovered that, instead of using the bank, money could be drawn through the Post Office without question and had started using that means, Seepy felt reasonably sure that the men would at least get the money the Government permitted them without any worrying delays. He set off in good spirits, which were in no way lowered when the man who had been trailing him like a wasp, ferreting into all his affairs, having got on his bike to continue his pursuit, was swallowed up in a cloud of dust as the vehicle suddenly accelerated along the sandy road. Seepy grinned broadly as he waved goodbye to his persecutor.

When he and Wilda arrived in Canton they made parcels of the warm clothing they no longer needed and put the remainder of their Chinese money into an envelope, and mailed it all back to Arthur. There was no more that he could do. He cheerfully waved aside the solicitous suggestions of the missionaries in Hongkong that he should take a rest, relax for a few days after all he'd been through, before going any farther. With a wife and three children in America, parents and a sister in England, what would he be doing kicking his heels in Hongkong? Two days after his arrival there he was on a plane, heading for home.

Arthur was just getting over the surge of relief he had known when Wilda and Lilah actually got safely away, and becoming aware of his own immediate needs again when the parcels of clothing and the money reached him. 'The clothes ... have proved a very productive source of supply,' he wrote later. 'I have been able to trade them for food, and the score to date is : over two hundred eggs, four hens, and bowls of milk galore', and when, in May, he received the allowance which Rupert sent through the Post Office, he knew he would no more have to face the humiliation of going to the Head of Police to get his permission to draw it from the bank.

The ordeal of this monthly application, which had to be made personally, had been perhaps the most acute trial of all, for the Head of Police hated him. There was a reason for it. Very soon after the Mathews' arrival in Hwangyuan the man had taken their cameras. Then a higher official had found out about it, and commanded him to return them. It had not been so much the loss of the cameras as the loss of face involved in giving them back that had implanted the implacable animosity in his heart against 'those imperialists' that revealed itself at every opportunity. The easy and obvious one was to refuse to grant the order to draw money. There had been times when Arthur had sat patiently, hour after hour, moulding balls of manure and coal dust to provide for his family the firing they could not afford to buy, and this he had done quite readily. The surprise of passers-by to see him engaged in such a degrading occupation had been as nothing compared to facing the snarling refusal to his request, of the man who loathed him. Arthur Mathews was a strong man, not the type that is easily intimidated, but he came back trembling on one occasion from the police station, where he had been violently threatened by the Head of Police and some twenty of his henchmen. He had stood his ground as they surrounded him, shouting, but:

'I feel I can't take that again,' he had said to Wilda when he got home, empty-handed still. As things turned out, he never had to. Next time he went the Head of Police was absent, and a stranger in his place granted the money without question. Now, with this new arrangement through the Post Office, he could always draw it without application to the Police Station.

As month succeeded month, however, he wondered how much longer he would have to be alone. He and Rupert were corresponding frequently, each conscious of the desire for the companionship of the other, but mid-June found them still in the same situation, and with no evidence that things would ever be different. Both had had a bout of sickness, and as Arthur wrote:

'When you don't feel too well, and have to potter around and keep wondering whether the medical book is right or wrong in guidance, then the days are inclined to drag.'
But in the same letter he added:

'On Saturday I read Luke 22.37 – "*The things concerning me have an end*", and it has been a growing seed of comfort in my mind since then . . . I'm not trying to fix any time-limit; we've learned that it is not given to us to know. "*It is not for you to know the times.*"

'But we can fix on facts. And the fact *is*, there *is* an end.'

It was almost as though he could hear it now, at a distance but coming nearer – the countdown.

With Rupert Clarke something of the sort was happening. Alone again, in Sining now, he realised that the anniversary of the opening of the clinic was drawing near. July 5. He always remembered the date, and the Lord always remembered it, too. He had no doubt of that. Would the Lord have an anniversary present for him again this year?

However, the day passed without incident. The solitary routine was just as it had been for the months since Seepy left, and since he did not know what was going on in Government offices in Peking, what reports being made, what records investigated, what laconic instructions given or urgent telephone calls made, what ripples of bureaucratic agitation were spreading out to the authorities in Tsinghai, he went to bed that night without any knowledge that things were heading up to a crisis. The time of his trial was running out now, and nothing could stop it.

In less than a week the police were at the door, telling

him to pack his bags, and accompany them to the police station.

The same day Arthur Mathews, in Hwangyuan, rose very early. He wanted to water the few vegetables he had planted in his little patch of ground before the burning heat of the sun got at them. His parsnips were doing well, he noted, and soon he'd have some fresh lettuce . . .

Then he became aware that someone was hurrying towards him. A policeman.

'Get your luggage together! Hurry up! Be ready to leave for Sining in an hour's time!'

Going to Sining? It took a moment or two for him to recover from the shock. Was this the first step to freedom? Or was it . . .? Anyhow, he'd better snatch some breakfast between packing, for who knew when he'd get his next meal?

His Bible! His passport! Razor, toothbrush, soap, towel, underclothes, bedding . . . What would he need, what should he take? Would he still be in China next winter, and need these wadded clothes, or could he leave them behind? As he hurried here and there the thought of Ben came riding up in his mind. Ben, the youngster who had stood by them through everything, deprived himself that Lilah might have the milk her parents could not afford to buy! It had all been so sudden and unannounced, Ben might not even know about the summons. Whatever else he did or failed to do, he must see Ben. How could he leave without saying goodbye? But he must do it secretly. If he was seen talking to the lad, there would be trouble for him later.

He went to the built-in cupboard and pulled out the drawer. They had early discovered that Ben's room was just beyond, and had managed to keep this means of communication secret.

'Ben! Ben! Are you there? They've come for me. I'm going. The Lord be with you, Ben. Here, take these,' and he pushed through what was left of his food stores. 'And this . . .' some of his own little fund of cash. 'We'll pray for each other, Ben. The Lord be with you . . .'

This was the painful thing about leaving Hwangyuan. The memory of the lad's face was to remain with Arthur long after other impressions had faded away, returning again and again down through the years as he knelt before God in prayer. But the emotion had to be choked back now, there must be no evidence given of the strength of the bond between them, or it would be the worse for Ben when he was gone. 'The Lord be with you!'

Down to the police station, and into a police van – not pushed into the back but in the best seat, in front beside the driver! 'This is the Lord's doing, and it is marvellous,' thought Arthur. Before midday he was in Sining, given something to eat, and led into a cell.

Rupert, in a cell opposite, caught a glimpse of him. 'That's Arthur!' he thought, his heart pounding. 'Things are looking up! We're on the move.'

Later that afternoon, as he was being escorted across to the law court, Arthur spotted Rupert having his luggage examined. He gave a loud cough – Rupert looked up, glanced in his direction, but prisoners with serious charges against them in Communist China have to be careful. They studiously avoided looking at each other. Arthur entered the law court, and stood before the judge. What were the charges against him, he wondered.

There were five. The first was collaboration in the murder of Dr. Kao of Changyeh, in 1936.

'In 1936 I was a student in Melbourne Bible Institute,' said Arthur firmly. 'I did not come to China until 1938.'

The judge was a little irritated about that, but after some rapid scribbling passed on to the next charges. When under the Nationalist regime Arthur Mathews had accused a girl to the authorities, saying she was a Communist. As a result she had been tortured and maimed for life. On a journey through China from Chefoo to Lanchow, he had spread sedition. By his photography and letters he had proved himself to be an imperialist. He had seized someone else's property.

Now all that was required of him was that he should sign a confession of these charges. Then he could leave the country, rejoin his wife and child in America.

Arthur refused to do so. 'They are not true,' he said.

The judge scolded, argued, shouted. But Arthur could shout, too.

'I stand before God and before you!' he cried. 'I deny all these charges. I will not sign.'

All right! He would not sign? Very well, he should be brought before the people! Let them decide what should be done with him! To Lanchow with him, for public trial. He was given to understand that it would include being paraded through the streets of Lanchow with a placard round his neck.

He was bundled into the back seat of a jeep, beside Rupert, to whom he was forbidden to speak, and taken to prison. They were put in separate cells, and next morning led off to the Civic Auditorium. Two Roman Catholic priests, westerners like themselves, were to be brought to trial as well, and Rupert was taken with them to face a vast crowd of people, while their crimes were read out for all to hear.

But not Arthur.

To his dismay, he was separated from them and taken off into a little room across the courtyard. 'Why?' he asked himself. This could only mean one thing. He was to be held back, a special case. The other three would be deported, and he would be left, the only member of C.I.M. still in China! He would much, much rather have been with them on the platform, facing that menacing crowd, than be here alone, with his paralysing fears.

Outside the trial was proceeding, and the prisoners' offences read out. Rupert was again accused of murder. It didn't seem to matter that this time the victim had died five years before Rupert had arrived. Amongst the charges levelled against the Roman Catholic priests was that one of them had been found to own some carpenters' tools, while posing as a holy man! Altogether, what was to be done with these wicked men?

'Deport them! Eternal deportation from China! To be put into effect immediately!'

The three prisoners looked duly lugubrious and downcast. They had learned to hide their feelings very thoroughly by this time.

A police official ran across the courtyard to the room where Arthur was waiting, and standing before him read from the sheet of paper he held in his hand. Again he was reading the charges against him. The first had been altered, however. It had been changed to 'In league with the murderer of Dr. Kao in 1948.' Having read them out the policeman folded up the paper, still unsigned, and shouted:

'Everlasting deportation! To be put into immediate effect.'

Reporters swarmed around and cameras clicked as the four men were hustled into a truck. It was all good copy for the newspapers. The deportees looked very unkempt and shabbily dressed.

Only Arthur was uneasy now. The other three had stood trial, but what about him! Was this another move in the cat-and-mouse game, and would he be held back at the last minute, while they were taken down to the border – and liberty. They spent the night in an inn, well guarded, and when, the following afternoon, a policeman came and told them to get ready to leave, the train would be going in about an hour, Arthur couldn't believe the order included him.

'But I thought you were going to have a special meeting to try me . . .?'

'Shut up!' hissed Rupert through his teeth.

It was very unlike Rupert. Arthur was so surprised that he shut up.

Then it began to dawn on him that he was included

in the general deportation order. There wasn't going to be a public trial for him, he wasn't going to be paraded round the streets, he wasn't going to be kept back while the others went on. They were all hustled into the train, six armed guards with revolvers accompanying them, and they were off.

They were held up once or twice – two days in Sian because the trains were so crowded, three days in Tienshui because the lines had to be repaired. In some ways it was quite a pleasant journey. There was no queuing for tickets or places on the train, as far as they were concerned. All arrangements were made for them, they had sleepers at night, they were given food. It was in Tienshui, however, that a memorable incident occurred. They were accommodated in the jail there, but the jailers were quite friendly, and when it came to dinner time one of them asked casually:

'What would you like to eat?'

The Roman Catholic priests were speechless. They had had quite a lot of experience in prisons by this time, but never anything like this. They were being asked what they would like to eat! In prison! They were too surprised to reply.

Arthur looked at the questioner blankly. He couldn't believe he had heard aright. After two and a half years of confrontations with the Head of Police in Hwangyuan, this couldn't be real! In any case, he couldn't think of anything.

Only Rupert kept his head. True to type, he reflected gravely for a moment, then calmly made his decision.

'What would you like to eat?'

When he answered, he spoke for them all. There had been very few pigs in Tsinghai, where they came from, it being a Muslim area, so he knew what they would like.

'Sweet and sour pork,' he said.

*   *   *

Arthur lay on his bunk with his eyes closed, but he was not asleep. Relief was ebbing up through him slowly, gently, easing the tension – he hadn't realised how taut he had been, sitting upright hour after hour on those hard wooden seats, until now. The loud-speakers with their incessant news and propaganda were silent at last, and the roar of the train was strangely soothing as metal rolled swiftly over metal, pistons throbbing as a hundred pieces of wood and metal straining and yielding blended together in a concerted movement onwards. How long it was since he had heard that rhythmic noise, felt the pull and the roll of a machine plunging steadily, accurately, along a well-laid track! He stretched himself cautiously, so as not to attract the suspicious eye of the armed guard, and listened to the familiar sound. The harsh, barren north-west was receding farther and farther into the distance, the years of living under the ominous threat of starvation, imprisonment, death by violence were nearly over. He was being borne along effortlessly in the very heart of the train as it sped through the night towards Hongkong, and its steady rumble was reassuring.

And through them all, the Lord had been with him.

Somehow he and Wilda had always been enabled to believe that, even when they had been puzzled, cast down, enveloped in the fear that seemed to pervade everything, tense with apprehension. '*I have prayed for thee, that thy faith fail not.*' Faith had not failed, though there had been times when very nearly everything else within them had. But there had been times, too, when faith and devotion had soared, as when they had come to the point of not only submitting to the will of God, but accepting it, delighting to do it, whatever might be the cost. The glory that had filled their souls then! And all along the pathway there had been the little tender tokens of His care and His compassion, sometimes in tangible form when needed provisions had come in the nick of time, sometimes in the deeper, indefinable way when His Word had spoken to their spirits. Through it all, the Lord had been with them.

Words were flowing quietly through his mind now, like a refreshing stream, as he lay on the hard bunk, the roar of the engines in his ears. Words that had taken on an intimate, personal meaning.

> *'As birds flying, so will the Lord of hosts defend Jerusalem; defending also he will deliver it; and passing over he will preserve it.'*

Defended. Delivered. Preserved.

Silently the healing tears began to flow . . .

The border. Long low buildings, barbed wire fences, the last Communist guards. Across an iron bridge, more barbed wire, more Chinese guards, but wearing a different uniform. The Union Jack fluttering on a pole above them.

'Your passports?'

'They took them from us, and didn't return them. We've been deported.'

An old Roman Catholic priest stepped forward. He met that train every day, had been doing so for years. He knew what would have to be done.

'Come and have something to eat and drink while they write you some temporary papers. Yes, I'll phone your people in Kowloon, and tell them you've arrived.'

The phone call was put through at five minutes to five on the afternoon of 20 July 1953. It had been a tiring day, and it was very hot and humid in the C.I.M. office. Albert Grant lifted the receiver rather wearily, then stiffened suddenly, listening incredulously to the message.

'Two of your people have just crossed the border. Dr. Rupert Clarke and Mr. Arthur Mathews.'

'Clarke and Mathews! Praise the Lord!' The ejaculation was involuntary.

'We've put them on the train to Kowloon. Goodbye.'

'They're out! Clarke and Mathews! Over the border!' Grant shouted. 'Coming in on the next train! Get ready!'

All was activity now, the heat and the weariness forgotten.

'We must get bedrooms ready – clear out that office – put the desk in the dining room, files in the hall. Move in two beds. Turn on the electric fan!'

'Phone the station – what time is the train due? We must all be there, waiting!'

When the train drew in at Kowloon station at five forty-five p.m. eager eyes scanned the passengers, searching for two westerners among the swarm of Chinese. There they were! Arthur smiling rather shyly, a cloth bag dangling from his shoulder, Rupert erect and doffing a trilby hat.

The C.I.M. had been safely withdrawn from China.

* * *

The cables went off an hour later. To South Africa, America, England, Australia, New Zealand – but first of all, to Singapore.

Arnold Lea was in his office when it arrived, and as soon as he grasped its message he leapt to his feet, hurried out into the corridor, and sounded the gong.

'They're out – Clarke and Mathews! Out at last, in Hongkong!' Then he added with a break in his voice:

'Let us all gather in the prayer hall, to give thanks to God.'

> 'How good is the God we adore,
>   Our faithful, unchangeable friend,
> Whose love is as great as His power
>   And knows neither measure nor end.
>
> 'Tis Jesus, the first and the last,
>   Whose Spirit shall guide us safe home,
> We'll praise Him for all that is past,
>   And trust Him for all that's to come.'

When the heart-felt prayers and the last joyous strains of the well-known, well-loved hymn had died away, he went back to his office, sat down at his desk, and put his head in his hands.

It was over. The long drawn out strain of uncertainty, the continual consciousness of those left still in China, the fear of what might be happening to them, had come to an end. The exodus was complete. That prayer of Mrs. Mason's 'Not a hoof nor a husband left behind' had been answered.

He didn't know whether he was laughing or crying as he thought of it. 'Not a hoof nor a husband!' It had been fulfilled quite literally. From that never-to-be-forgotten occasion when it had been decided to withdraw the Mission, right through till now, not one member had died in China, nor one member had emerged maimed, not one member had been left behind. There had been deaths in the Mission by accident, by sudden heart attack, by normal illness and old age *outside* of China during those years, but none inside. All had come safely out.

He must let everybody else know immediately – Bishop Houghton and J.R.S. especially. And the superintendents in the new fields; Kuhn in Thailand, Leonard Street in Japan, Broomhall and Toliver in the Philippines, Williamson in Malaya, Stead in Indonesia . . . They'd all been involved in the withdrawal, all carried the thought of their colleagues still in China in their hearts. He must let them know.

When the messages were all sent he opened a drawer in his desk and drew out the large sheet of paper on which had been typed the names of those 627 who were in China at the beginning of 1951. Through the months and the years, as news had come of those crossing the border, he had put his pencil through the names, and at the bottom of the page totted up the number still remaining.

He looked at the last entries. How laconic were those entries, and how little they revealed of all that lay behind them! But God knew each tiny detail, each victory of faith, each earnest prayer. And the times had been in His hands.

    1952.   22 May 8
    1953.   1 Jan. 4
    1953.   24 March ... 2

Now, in the bottom right hand corner of the great sheet he wrote:

    1953.   20 July ...... ZERO.

Then he bowed his head, and worshipped.

A few months later an Australian couple, Harry and Elizabeth Gould, employed by the shipping firm Butterfield and Swire in Shanghai, applied for their exit visas, wound up their affairs, packed their bags and emerged uneventfully from China. Now that everyone in the C.I.M. was safely out, they felt the time had come to take a holiday.

Epilogue

BY ARNOLD LEA

And so ends the thrilling account of yet another great deliverance under the mighty Hand of our God. He planned, He protected and He provided for each of the over 600 members of the Mission who were in China when the decision to withdraw was taken. Not a life nor a limb was lost. To God be the glory. Amen.

It was the end of the C.I.M. in China, but not the end for the churches of God in China. For them it marked a new beginning. With a deep sigh of relief and thanksgiving we missionaries one by one crossed the bridge that marked the border between China and Hongkong. But it was with heavy hearts that we thought of our Chinese brothers and sisters left behind to face the fiery furnace of persecution. Two years under a Communist government had given us an insight into the ruthlessness and determination of the new leadership. While the Constitution upholds religious freedom, it also maintains the liberty to oppose religious faith. And so the furnace becomes seven times fiercer. It was with just a situation in mind that our Lord had said, 'On this rock I will build my Church and the gates of Hell shall not prevail against it.'

We must not let the word 'Church' conjure up for any of us a place of worship made of wood or stone. The only Church in China is a 'building not made with hands,' consisting of living stones, Christ Jesus being the chief corner stone. He would be with them in the fiery furnace. And so the Church was forced to go out of sight. Not as some have thought, to become a 'secret church' – far from that, as individuals make opportunities to pass on the Good

News to others. Nor is the term 'underground' really acceptable, for this might suggest subversive activities. The Church of God in China is a Hidden Church; its activities have to be undertaken out of sight. Far more precious is the thought found in Isiah 49:2, where the Lord hides away His own, until the time for which He is preparing.

> . . . in the shadow of His Hand He hid me
> He made me a polished arrow,
> In His quiver He hid me away.

God's Sovereign purpose is that His Church in China may be like a polished arrow, kept hidden in the quiver close at His side until the day when He would bring it forth.

Opposition to Christianity fluctuated in severity until the time of the Cultural Revolution, when all the powers of Hell were let loose. Mao's Red Guards saw to it that not a single church building escaped closure or confiscation, while every religious book they could discover was burned and the Christian was held up to ridicule. Although under these pressures some Christians failed in the hour of testing, for the majority persecution only made them more determined to live for Christ. A Christian whose husband had previously been killed for belonging to the landlord class, herself came under fire some years later. She was cruelly treated, beaten and her head completely shaved. Her answer was daily to climb the ladder into the loft, there to spend from dawn to dusk copying out by hand the Chinese Bible. The latest news her daughter received said that she had completed once through from Genesis to Revelation, and was starting on the second copy! Such is the hunger engendered amongst believers for the precious Word of God.

Normally, Christians have to be very careful what they write in letters going abroad. One who had been converted through listening to a Christian radio broadcast wrote of his new-found joy. The letter was intercepted by the censor and the writer clapped into prison. At other times letters came through uncensored. One such was written by a young man to his father, whom he had never seen. He had been born 24 years before, when his father was attending meetings outside of China and never got back home. This letter told of a recent experience when he had found Christ as Saviour. Completely uninhibited by any thought of censorship, he wrote in glowing praise of what God had just done for him. Such happenings remind us that God is alive in China today.

It is significant that several who had never had any Christian teaching in all their lives, when in desperate situations instinctively put up a prayer to the God they had been taught to discountenance. Those escaping by the sea route to Hongkong first had ardous journeys overland, walking by night and hiding up during the daylight hours. Delays along the way often resulted in running out of food. One such situation faced an ex-Red Guard on his way to the coast. He put up a prayer to the 'unknown God' to help him. Shortly afterwards, he and his companion came across a hidden cache of sweet potatoes. When eventually he reached Hongkong he set out to find a Christian who would explain more fully the reality of the God who had answered his prayer. Soon after he was rejoicing in Christ as his Saviour.

The Gospel has prevailed over the powers of Hell, not only sustaining believers but winning non-Christians. A Christian doctor working in a government hospital openly witnessed to his faith in Christ. The authorities did not remove him for he was needed for his professional brilliance, but they did plan to make him change his beliefs. A nurse, well trained in such tactics, was drafted to that hospital with the express purpose of undermining his Christian stand. She first made friends with him and then set out through argument to destroy his faith. Soon she found she was being challenged by all that he said in reply, until the day came when she found she must believe in this one true God. Her conversion to Christ made quite a stir, and more so when she married the one she had come to destroy. The authorities, nonplussed, sent the couple down to the country to work. Here, too, they found opportunities to witness for Christ.

It is not only conversions which are indicative of God's working in China. Christians have enjoyed the fullness of life in Christ and have found new meaning to prayer. A young man in Hongkong received a letter from the far interior of China telling of the death of his grandmother at the age of over eighty. She had been bedridden for the last nine years and spent much of each day pleading with God for revival in the province.

Though Christians were called to suffer in the normal way with their countrymen, yet there have been reports of God's sovereign intervention – miracles of healing, of exorcism and of special protection given to those meeting in His Name. A Baptism service was planned for early morning on the top of a lonely mountain. Somehow the police heard of this plan and early on the morning of the baptisms they set out by truck. Halfway up it broke down, and they had to proceed on foot. As they drew near to the summit they saw the area surrounded by Government troops and decided to return to base. Later it was reported that no soldiers had been in the vicinity at that time! As with Elisha and his servant, so God's guardian angels had been sent, this time dressed to look like soldiers! The day of miracles is not past.

During these twenty-six years such a variety of reports have filtered out, that it would be impossible to form any composite picture. Then again, Christians from Hongkong and elsewhere who have gone in to see their relatives bring out different if not contradictory pictures of life in China. Some report the people as happy, others as sad. Some report the common people as being well clothed and well fed, others just the opposite. Some have not met up with even one Christian, others have made contact with several. Most areas report Christians as forced to meet in twos and threes, but in one area whole villages are Christian, and in another over a hundred were baptised in a week. Each bit of news must be recognised as an isolated incident and not for generalisation. However, with such a vast land as China and knowing the mighty power of the Holy Spirit, should we not anticipate that what we know is happening in one place is being duplicated in other provinces also?

Structured Church life has been swept away, denominational barriers have crumbled, laymen are sharing responsibilities since pastors have had to earn a living. Evangelistic meetings have given way to personal evangelism. Small house meetings have superseded larger gatherings for worship. The shortage of Bibles has brought a renewed hunger for the Word of God. Christ has become so real and His Coming earnestly expected.

Great changes have recently been taking place in the whole manner of living. A new spirit of enquiry is blowing through the student world, coupled with some measure of relaxation from above. This is affecting politics, education, industry and agriculture. But most striking is the new attitude towards foreign visitors. Barring another revolution, communication may well improve rapidly. Access to China is proving increasingly easy and holds out hopes of freer communication between Christians in China and those in other parts of the world. Already, thousands of Chinese students are designated to study in western universities. It may not be long before Christians from the Third World and from western countries are allowed to enter and extend the right hand of fellowship. Even more exciting is the thought of Christians from within coming out to share with us the wonderful lessons they have learned from God during these twenty-six years of being refined in the crucible of suffering. Happy, indeed, is the thought that we may have the privilege of sitting at their feet while they share with us treasures both old and new.